"In this book there are

from his many experien

God to His Word. When ... spoke to him telling him what to do. When he obeyed the voice of God, miracles were performed. Thank God for a man who is willing to obey, regardless how foolish it may sound at the time. 'Faith without works is dead.' James 2:17."

Houston Miles, Founder, Chairman,
Evangel Fellowship Internationa,
Spartanburg, South Carolina

"Venture into the unknown. Step out by Faith to a brave new world! Cornelius Joubert records the fantastic journey he and his family traveled for many years. It was not simply the journey from lay leadership in South Africa to evangelism in America. It was more so the exhilarating journey of faith from spiritual novice to master warrior in the Army of God. In this book, Brother Corrie tells of his work in the 'Kingdom of God,' not only as a royal ambassador of the Heavenly King, but also as a secret agent, commissioned by the Commanding General, assigned to battle the forces of Hell and work the work of Heaven. The record of this remarkable crusade teaches valuable lessons of faith and obedience. These lessons are now ready to be transposed upon the reader of this book by the power of the Holy Spirit. As you read *Two Invisible Kingdoms,* invite the Holy Spirit that has kept, strengthened, enlightened, and taught Brother Corrie over the past many years to equip, enable, and energize you to fight the Good fight of Faith!"

Bishop Kenneth D. Baker,
Sr., State Overseer of the Church of God of Prophecy,
South Carolina

"This book is very inspiring and it will help to strengthen your faith in your walk with God. It's filled with miracles performed by God for a man who is rich in faith and rich in God."

Rev. and Mrs. Barry Manley

"This book reminds me that God is a 'Today' God and that signs and wonders occur in this day and age. I read this book in two days and it was hard for me to stop until it was completed. The scripture references proved to me that God's promises are true."

Jeanette Pinion,
Medical Laboratory Technician

"*Two Invisible Kingdoms* is an inspirational story of faith and courage in the face of adversity. You will be blessed—and challenged—as you read the stories of faith in action. I highly recommend *Two Invisible Kingdoms.*"

Barbara Johnson, Executive Assistant to Dr. Pat Robertson,
The Christian Broadcasting Network,
Virginia Beach, VA

"A blessing to read. When I started reading it, I didn't want to stop. The kids also loved it when I told them the testimonies!"

Sister June, Children's Pastor

"We have read this inspiring book and received a great blessing. My soul was truly inspired as I read the experiences this man and his wife had with God. May God continue to bless them as they move forward in their relationship with Him."

James and Ruby Jesseff

"I truly enjoyed this book. There are no limits as to what God is able to do, if we will just humble ourselves and believe. Always put Him first, because through God's grace and love He will strengthen us. With Him all things are possible."

Linda Morgan

"It made me laugh and cry and really lifted my spirit to higher heights in the Lord. In *Two Invisible Kingdoms* I have seen God work miracles."

Mrs. Roberta Reid

"After reading *Two Invisible Kingdoms* and learning Mr. Joubert's stand on faith, the enemy attacked me with sickness. I decided to take God on His Word as he did and He healed me. Thank you!"

John Carpenter

"It inspired me so much, I went and bought ten more to give to my friends. Thank you and God bless you."

Ruby Owens

2

INVISIBLE KINGDOMS

INVISIBLE KINGDOMS

The Supernatural Nature of Everyday Life

†

CORRIE JOUBERT

Tate Publishing & *Enterprises*

Two Invisible Kingdoms: The Supernatural Nature of Everyday Life

Published by Tate Publishing & Enterprises, LLC
127 E. Trade Center Terrace | Mustang, Oklahoma 73064 USA
1.888.361.9473 | www.tatepublishing.com

Tate Publishing is committed to excellence in the publishing industry. The company reflects the philosophy established by the founders, based on Psalms 68:11,
"The Lord gave the word and great was the company of those who published it."

Cover design by Lindsay Behrens
Interior design by Jennifer Redden

Published in the United States of America

ISBN: 978-1-60247-543-4
07.06.13

From outer space we are controlled by forces unseen-*Light and Darkness. The Force of Darkness:* invades without permission. It is destructive in its very nature. The objective of this force is to create disruption of nations, families and people; to introduce unproductive behavior, division, hatred, un-forgiveness, self pity, destructive habits and the list goes on and on. *The Force of Light:* Works oppositely. It seeks permission without invasion. It offers wisdom, health, wealth, and protection from the *Force of Darkness.* The eternal purpose of the *Force of Light* is to prepare for a future Kingdom that offers eternal peace and wellbeing. It exists exclusively to enhance the human race to a higher level.

Acknowledgment

I dedicate this book to my wife, Genevieve. Together we decided to work for the kingdom of God, and she has been by my side ready in season, and ready out of season. Together we have worked to the furthering of the Kingdom we chose together, however small a part our efforts played, we did it, nevertheless. My beloved wife, I appreciate you more than you can ever realize. At times things were difficult, especially those times when I was gone from my family, yet you never complained. Thank you for always being there. I also thank my children, Virginia, Gillian, Gordon and Michael. Today I thank God that all my children are stable individuals and assets to the Invisible Kingdom and to society in their own individual ways, and I am very proud of each one of them.

Contents

Foreword

When Corrie first asked me to write a foreword to the re-publication of his book (originally titled *God's Secret Agent "008": Exposing Mysteries from God's Invisible Kingdom*), I was both honored and humbled. Honored because of the long-standing friendship and his respect for my giftings (which, as most of us do, I often question), and humbled because I don't begin to feel that I have the level of faith he and Genny demonstrate in their journey. I covet such faith (Paul tells us to "covet earnestly the best gifts") and find in these two friends of God a model to emulate, as well as a source of thankfulness to our Father for placing someone like them in our lives.

As I write this, I am in my third reading. The first was a number of years ago, and though I admired the journey of faith I saw, it was at a distance, and perhaps in my mind at the time, unattainable for me personally. When I found the book at a used book sale recently, I immediately bought it, but it was still a number of months before I picked it up again. By that point, I had "ripened" and was far more ready for what I encountered. Now, as I am reading it again, I am often moved to tears, as I can so fully relate to the concepts Corrie has fleshed out-talking to God as an intimate friend, being cared for by a totally loving and good Father, not worrying about how God will take care of details in accomplishing what He has committed to in our lives.

And I have known Corrie and Genny through some of their recent hard times. My wife and I try to meet with them weekly for prayer, though our schedules so often mitigate against it that it's more like monthly. Still, each time with them is fresh, and they are so willing to receive as well as to give. I have watched them struggle through trying to understand why he had to endure a major operation when they believe so radically in healing and have seen and felt the Spirit move in such incredible power. Though they are well advanced in years, they have opted to foster some very troubled and abused young girls, fighting for them through prayer, worship and deliverance in the midst of the demonic lions' dens these precious children have been thrown into-in the process earning high accolades from the decidedly non-religious authorities who control the girls' destinies.

And yet they are still just our friends, who get frustrated as we do, hurt as we do, stretch for heaven's best as we do. They know as well as anyone that it's about the journey, and it's not over till it's over. We all still have to run the specific race laid out for us; no one can do that for us. But as you read, enter into their journey, and let it make your steps a little lighter as they share your burdens, feel your broken heart, urge you onward to excellence. Until we finish, we're on a level playing field, and there's no way we can win the game alone. We are meant to "spur one another on to love and good deeds," to "encourage one another while it is still called 'Today'," to cheer and rejoice and cry and hurt with each other.

There is really only "Today," only this moment. Someone has said, "Yesterday is a cancelled check; tomorrow is a promissory note." Someone else has said, or should say, "Yesterday is only a shadow, tomorrow only a dream." When Jesus performed His first miracle of turning water into wine (John 2), He was totally into the moment. It appears from His response to His mother that He was not really ready to help out in such a way: "My time is not yet." And yet, when she ignored Him and told the servants to do whatever He said, somehow He got in touch with His Father, and His time "came." Corrie and Genny have lived this sort of "moment-specific obedience" in ways we can more easily relate to-when the car is almost out of gas and there's no hope of gas in the foreseeable future or distance; when what the Father is calling you to seems so far out that you simply have to put one foot in front of the other; when you have to ask without any basis of knowing that you will receive an answer or where the source of that answer will come from.

"What do we have that we are not given?" We are all given a measure of faith, and Corrie and Genny have been faithful farmers, sowing in season, watering and tending, hoeing and weeding, waiting and watching for the crops. They are still in process, as we all are. Take these faithful farmers' almanac and learn to plant your own mustard-seed acorns and watch them grow into towering oaks of strength and shade. They have been servants called to the harvest in the early morning, and have borne the heat of the day; but even if it's the eleventh hour, your faithfulness in that last hour of the harvest can receive the same reward.

Ken Stewart

Founder and CEO of Easley Electric Corporation

The Spirit Who Outsmarted Scientists

And Joseph said unto Pharaoh, the dream of Pharaoh is one: God hath showed Pharaoh what He is about to do.

Genesis 41:25

My thoughts went back to 1972, when I worked as a Nutritional Scientist for the Cape Provincial Hospitals in South Africa.

One of the many questions people have asked me over the many years in full-time ministry is, "How does God speak to us?" My answer is plain and simple, God speaks to us in that still small voice, that same still small voice that is on the inside of every child of God. The problem of feeling alone, or not feeling that God is near us is due to the fact that we have often enough ignored the voice of the Holy Spirit to the point where we no longer hear Him. When that happens one has to almost start over again and relearn and develop our communication with our heavenly Father. My sincere desire is that in the pages of this book some may find that the secrets of the invisible kingdom are not so secret. In fact, it is all around us, and in us. God wants to stay in touch and communicate with His children. What keeps us from entering into daily communication with our Spiritual Father is our own alienation of God. It is we who neglect to allow the Holy Spirit time to direct our lives, our business, our pleasures. It is not God's fault if we can't hear Him. Mistakenly many of God's precious children have the erroneous idea that the church is the place where they should get God's direction or hear from God. However, that is not the biblical example. Jesus said to the woman at the well:

> Woman, believe me, the hour is coming when neither on this mountain nor in Jerusalem will you worship the Father. You worship what you do not know; we worship what we know, for salvation is from the Jews. But the hour is coming, and now is, when the true worshipers will worship the Father in Spirit and truth, for such the Father seeks to worship Him. God is a Spirit, and they that worship Him must worship Him in Spirit and in truth.
>
> John 4:21–24 RSV

Worshiping God is not necessarily something one does in a specific place. Neither is worshiping God something one does in particular exercise. Rather we ought to think of worship as a relationship, or adoration, or ones whose company we prefer. The dictionary defines worship as intense love and admiration. Davis Dictionary of the Bible defines worship as respect and honor shown to a person. Worship then becomes a state of mind for the believer to whom God has become his everything. God becomes a part of one's life, as stated in Acts 17:28: "In Him we live and move and have our being; as even some of your poets have said; for we are indeed His offspring."

If I am an offspring then I have to realize that I am totally dependent on my Father for my life, my success, my health and everything in life I decide to do. Why then do so many of God's people have such a hard time? Why do so many of God's people feel so alienated? My answer is simple. If we are serious enough and patient enough to want to hear God speak to us, then we must take time to involve Him, and allow Him access into our busy lives.

Consider these words of Jesus:

> I have yet many things to say to you, but you can not bear them now. When the Spirit of truth [the Holy Spirit] comes He will guide you into all the truth; for He will not speak of His own authority, but whatever He hears He will speak, and He will declare to you the things that are to come. He will glorify me, for He will take what is mine and declare it to you. All that the Father has is mine; therefore I said that He will take what is mine and declare it to you.
>
> John 16:12–15 RSV

Since all knowledge belongs to the Father, and since Jesus has authorized the Holy Spirit to declare it to us, it only makes sense that I should draw on His knowledge. It was God who gave Noah the blueprint to build the world's first ship. It was God who directed Joseph on how to save the grain and feed the people of Egypt during the seven year drought.

It was God who directed Daniel to direct the king's business. There are too many examples in God's word to allow me the space to even mention but a few. The point here is that God has always involved Himself with His children. God is also the one who has given our world all the technology we have today. The Spirit of God said, "But thou O Daniel, shut up the words, and seal the book, even to the time of the end; many shall run to and fro, and knowledge shall be increased" (Daniel 12:4).

The word of God has declared the time we are living in today the end of time. There has never been a time like the time we are living in. Knowledge has exploded across the United States and the world. Daily our news media carries new discoveries, new breakthroughs in technology and medicine, etc.

It was the spring of 1971, and I was in the Republic of South Africa working for the Cape Provincial Hospital Services. I was one of a team of three who were overseeing the operations of the food service departments of thirty-five state-owned hospitals. As one of the three top managers directing the food service for these hospitals, it was my job to visit hospitals wherever there was over spending, or problems that needed to be addressed. I liked my job and was always taking great pride in my assignments.

One day I received a call from one of my associates, and was told that I had to report to the chief executive director of the Cape Provincial Hospital services. I did as I was told the next day and was told the following by the chief: "For two years we've had a team of scientists researching the feasibility of freezing food, developing a technology to freeze food, developing a technology to reconstitute food, and distributing and serving food via a multiple choice menu system. The problem we have encountered is we have not been able to develop any kind of gravies or sauces. We have developed a system to freeze the food, but still have to find a way to reconstitute the food. On top of all of that we also still have to develop a system of distribution. You are here today because we want you to go and find solutions for some of the undeveloped areas."

Wow! By the time I left his office, my head was spinning. I said, "Jesus, please get me out of this, I can't do it, I don't want to do it, I have no idea what has been done so far." However, all my complaining did nothing to change the situation. The Holy Spirit said to me to go and do it and to draw strength from Him.

The problems that were described to me were actually overwhelming. I wondered why they even wanted to continue. For the next couple of days I used my time to read over the results to date with the help of two assistants who also helped to inform me of the accomplishments to date.

Proverbs 3:6 says, "In all thy ways acknowledge Him, and He will direct thy paths." I regret that I waited to my middle thirties before learning about the power of acknowledging the Lord in my day-to-day activities. Even after I learned that it was to my own benefit to acknowledge the Lord in everything, I still neglected to do it on a regular basis.

The days went by fast and I started to do some experiments of my own with the help of my two assistants. However, in making the gravies, the results I got were no different than the researchers who were there before me. The problem with the gravies I found was that freezing them at extremely cold temperatures of three hundred degrees below zero resulted in the separation of the product's ingredients. I asked the Lord to please help me to find a solution. The next day while working on more experiments, a salesman walked in and tried to sell me a soup base he said his company developed. After he was done with his sales pitch I politely told him that he was wasting his and my time since this was a research unit and not a hospital kitchen. The salesman got the message, gathered up his stuff, and left without another word. However, he was no sooner out the door when the Holy Spirit said to me, "Why do you ask me to help you, and when I send you the help you asked for, you send him away?"

I said, "Lord, surely you don't mean the soup salesman?"

The Holy Spirit said, "That is exactly who I mean. The ingredient that you need to stabilize your gravies is in the soup mix." I could feel my stomach making a back flip. I ran out as fast as I could, leaving my two assistants without any explanation, to try and catch the salesman before he left. In my rudeness towards him he did not leave me his business card, and I did not pay attention to what he said, and had no idea what company he represented.

As I turned the corner of the building I could see him just getting ready to open his car door. I shouted and waved my hands to get his attention. Fortunately he heard me and waited. Out of breath I caught up with him and said, "I changed my mind, I will take one five gallon container of every flavor of the soup mix you have." The salesman looked at me in unbelief. He may have wanted to say more than he did, but all he said was, "Are you sure?"

I replied, "Yes, I am sure."

After the cases of soup mix were delivered my assistants and I began putting together mixes, blending flavors to see what kinds of different tasting gravies and sauces could be created. The results we achieved were actually very good. During the process my two assistants, who said they were Christians, wanted to know how I knew that it was God who told me to do what I did. They must have thought to themselves, "What kind of a nut case are we working with now?" One said to me, "I did not know that God still spoke to people. I thought that was only something that happened in the Bible. I did not think it was taking place today."

The true facts are that there are more people that are intimately conversing with God at this time in history than all the recorded instances in the Bible put together. To many it might not sound too scientific to conduct and experiment on information one received from listening to a little voice only you heard by someone no one else could see. But God is the One who has put the system in place. He is the One who decided how the system should work. I am not the one calling the shots. I am, however, a recipient of God's devoted love and undying interest in everything I do.

After we spent a day combining all kinds of flavors, we were ready to freeze our product. We began to run our experiment through what we called a freezing tunnel, which is nothing more than a stainless steel cover over a stand with a conveyor belt that feeds the product through. Little tiny jets running across the stainless steel cover that sprays liquid nitrogen at a controlled rate directly over the piping hot product. At temperatures of three hundred degrees below zero, it only takes about ten minutes to freeze the product solid. It is then stored at twenty degrees below zero. After we froze our products, we stored our product and called it a day.

The following morning we began the procedure of reconstituting the gravies. The test would show if the product stood up to the grueling cold temperatures, or reconstitute to the same consistency as it had before the freezing process. Our anticipation to see the results climaxed the air. Even my two assistants who questioned my sanity the day before were waiting with anticipation to see the results. After reconstituting the gravies we tested the quality and re-usability, taste and consistency. The results were perfect! So perfect, I could hardly believe that what I was looking at could not have been achieved before. All I could say was, "Thank you, Jesus." We, the Holy Spirit and I, just had the breakthrough in two weeks from the time I started there, which the team before me could not get in the previous two years. How good is God to His servants? He is very good.

Now since I had the breakthrough for the gravy, the Holy Spirit said to me, "You will have to change the way you prepare all your meals." For the next several weeks I followed the cooking procedures the Holy Spirit gave me and completely changed the way food was prepared in the conventional way. After six weeks we had progressed to the point of actually testing the food in a hospital setting, letting the patients eat it. But cautiously, the administration called a team of professional tasters to eat a meal with us to evaluate the food first. Their conclusion? "We have never tasted any food before that is as good as this."

Six weeks after I started my research we were given a hospital floor of patients to use to test the food on. The patients were not told anything and since they were long term patients, their intake was recorded every meal time. The results after thirty days? The hospital staff had recorded a fifty to one hundred percent better intake from our food than food that was prepared in a conventional hospital setting. How good is God? He is very good! Soon after the results were made known, I had other food scientists from other countries visiting to evaluate what we were doing. Three months later the administration decided to proceed and build a factory kitchen that could prepare and freeze fifteen to twenty thousand meals in an eight hour workday. The administration also decided to send all the chefs and dietitians from all thirty-five hospitals to my unit for retraining. The decision was based on our test results, that the methods I was using was more productive, healthier, and better accepted by patients.

God also did something else for me. I started to get two identical pay checks every month. Since the government was not in the business of giving employees bonuses, they decided to pay me double. However, the paymaster's office would always deny that they gave me two checks. When I called and said there were two checks in my envelope, they would deny knowing anything about it, but the checks kept coming for about six months. How good is God? God our Father is a very good God. We read in Genesis 41:39–40:

> And Pharaoh said to Joseph, for as much as God has showed thee all this, there is none so discreet and wise as thou art: Thou shalt be over my house, and according unto thy word shall all my people be ruled: only in the throne shall I be greater than thou.

It was certainly not Joseph's smarts that placed him second in command of all of Egypt. It was God's direction in Joseph's life. It was Joseph being faithful to God during his trial period. It was Joseph who did not get bitter because he was treated unfairly. Instead of accepting rejection and becoming bitter, Joseph continued to do the best he could do under the circumstances and continued his relationship with his God.

Remember that circumstances can't get us down, unless we give up and lose hope. To all the people like Joseph who are out there working against the tide of life, seemingly doing the best they can while nothing works out quite right, Jesus is saying,

> Come to me, all you who labor and are heavy laden and burdened, and I will cause you to rest - I will ease and relieve and refresh your souls. Take my yoke upon you and learn of me: For I am gentle [meek] and humble [lowly] in heart, and you will find rest - relief ease and refreshment and recreation and blessed quiet for your souls. For my yoke is wholesome [useful, good] not harsh, hard, sharp or pressing, but comfortable, and gracious and pleasant: and my burden is light and easy to born.
>
> Matthew 11:28–30 AMP

Right there is your and my personal invitation from the mastermind of the universe to come and ask for help. It is our invitation to allow Him, the King of kings, the opportunity to guide us and direct us in our daily activities. Taking a little time to ask Him how, may save us from making costly mistakes and developing a life of pain, rejection, depression and that feeling of being unfulfilled. How can anyone reject an invitation like that? This is the same invitation God gave Israel in Deuteronomy 28, offering to bless them, to make them successful, wealthy and keep them healthy. Sadly they did what numerous of God's people do today. Just like Israel stopped in the wilderness once they were saved from Egypt, Christians stop at salvation, completely disregarding God's invitation to walk and talk with us every day of our lives. Sometimes we try to fix our own problems rather than handing our problems to the master creator who already has the answer for us!

Intervention from Outer Space

> Now unto Him that is able to do exceeding abundantly above all that we ask or think, according to the power that worketh in us.
>
> Ephesians 3:20

Towards the latter part of 1972, after all my successes in developing the food freezing technology, the administration one day told me that they wanted my input into the design of the new factory hospital kitchen. They had plans for me to spend a couple of months in Germany to study kitchen designs and select the equipment that would be best suited for our facility. However, at the same time the Lord said to me, "I want you to get ready to go to Bible college."

First of all I had no idea where to find a Bible college. Personally I saw no reason for going. Genny and I were already busy night after night running a coffee shop in down town Cape Town City to reach people for Christ. We mostly attracted young night club goers. Genny and I were on a spiritual high, which kept us energized. Together with a friend we kept the coffee shop open five nights a week. So I said to the Lord, "I don't need to go to

Bible college because I was happy with my life, and want to leave it just the way it is."

It all started after I received the baptism of the Holy Spirit. Genny and I were invited to go to an all-day prayer session. The hours of prayer were most boring to say the least. That was until it came to my turn to pray. We had been there about five hours, and everyone got a chance to pray out loud. From the corner of my eye I tried to peek from underneath my arm to see who was praying. I first thought of going for a walk so I would not have to pray. I was quite sure that I was not the only one bored to death. I did not really want to pray; on the other hand I did not want to give a bad impression either. However, I waited too long, and suddenly the man next to me nudged me and said, "It is your turn."

It was perhaps because I was nervous, or maybe because I have been complaining to the Lord about how boring the prayer meeting was, and why was I wasting my time even being there. I don't know how it happened, but as I opened my mouth, it felt like my whole inside came flooding out through my mouth. I was babbling in a language other than the three I was familiar with. On top of that my body suddenly went into what felt like convulsions. I tried to steady myself from shaking out of control by getting a tighter grip on the bench where I was kneeling. The power of the Holy Spirit caused me to shake violently, to where the other brothers who were kneeling at the same bench backed away. The words I spoke came flooding out of me like an unstoppable flood. I don't know just how long that lasted, perhaps about five or ten minutes, when it stopped just as sudden as it came. I said, "Amen." And felt like the biggest fool one could possibly feel. After I quieted down, everyone continued in the same boring mode as they were before, as if nothing happened. I felt like crawling under something, but there was nowhere to hide. Later, on the way home, as Genny and I were driving back in the same car as the pastor, he casually commented. "I think you received the baptism in the Holy Ghost today."

> And they were filled with the Holy Spirit and began to speak in other tongues, as the Spirit gave them utterance.
>
> Acts 2:4, RSV

Well, whatever God gave me I knew it was something good even though I felt like crawling under the bench. As the days passed my obsession to do something for the Lord intensified. I assumed that the Holy Spirit baptism had something to do with that. Our coffee shop was not drawing a lot of people and we prayed for God to send us more souls. One night my friend said that the Lord had told him what to do to get more converts. He said we were supposed to go to the night club across the street and lay hands on the entrance door of the night club. That sounded good to me. I suggested everyone go lay hands on the night club while I stayed and monitored the coffee shop. I could see what they were doing from the second floor of the coffee shop. I did not mind them doing it at all. From where I was watching I could see the whole ridiculous scene. I figured that the Lord knew that I still had my pride and a reputation of sorts. I could not even imagine what people who walked by must have thought about it. I thought to myself that what they were doing did not seem logical at all, why would God have told him to do that? Or perhaps He did not. But this doubting Thomas was in for the surprise of a lifetime.

No more than one hour after they had laid their hands on and prayed over the door of the night club, a group of young men came marching up the stairs into the coffee shop. I can't remember who gave their testimony first that night, but about thirty or so minutes after these young men came in one of them said that he was the leader of the band that was playing every night at the club, and that he was tired of the kind of life he lived. He then said he wanted to accept Jesus Christ as his Savior and not play at the club any more. After we prayed with him, all of his group got up and said that they also wanted to accept Jesus and become born again. Ridiculous or not, my friend's strategy worked and God certainly honored his faith. Then the strangest thing of all happened. The band decided that God would not approve of them playing at the night club, and they asked if they could play for the coffee house. They went and got their instruments, and the fun started as we tried to teach them choruses.

They were able to learn the Christian songs fairly easily and that was when we had the bright idea to open the second floor windows. The sound from the band, now our band, traveled down the road, and thoroughly confused the party goers who were looking for the night club. The result was that many people who were not looking for us wandered in by mistake. Suddenly we were very busy giving testimony and ministering to people all the time. Almost every night someone was saved.

Why were we suddenly so successful in the outreach of the coffee house? Nothing much happened until the Holy Spirit injected the wisdom of God into our efforts. It was like the Lord was saying to us, "You are doing my work. Please don't tune me out. Let me help you." And that was exactly what He did.

From The Invisible Kingdom A Call For Service

While Apollos was at Corinth, Paul passed through the upper country and came to Ephesus. There he found some disciples. And he said to them, Did you received the Holy Spirit when you believed? And they said, No, we have never even heard that there is a Holy Spirit. And he said, Into what then were you baptized? They said, John baptized us with the baptism of repentance, telling people to believe in the one who was to come after him, that is Jesus. On hearing this they were baptized in the name of the Lord Jesus. And when Paul had laid his hands on them, the Holy Spirit came on them; and they spoke with tongues and prophesied. There were about twelve of them in all.

Acts 19:1–7 RSV

It always amazes me how we can complicate things for ourselves and how God will sometimes just use the simple things to get His message across. That is exactly how I describe this next event. My friend and I who were both members of the Full Gospel Business Men's Fellowship International, were informed that an airlift from the USA to South Africa had been planned. We did not want to miss out on the event. However, we had a problem. In Cape Town City there was not a chapter, and in order to have some of the members of the airlift team visit our city we had to have a chapter. We decided to use the coffee shop as a base and enroll the new converts into chapter members. Next I had to fly to Johannesburg to attend a meeting where all the details of the airlift were going to be made known to the South African Chapter presidents. We were informed that Cape Town City would host five of the American team members. The event had to be kicked off with a banquet. The duration of their stay would be for one week, and we had to get them speaking engagements for the seven days.

The events that followed I can only describe as awesome, considering the fact that my friend and I, both novices, were fumbling in the dark so to speak. Everything we did was the first time for both of us. We secured our reservations for the banquet at Cape Town's plush Plaza Hotel for two hundred. Then, my friend and I set out to sell two hundred tickets. I like to think about it as launching an assault on the enemy, trashing as much of the enemy territory as we could by reaching people with Christ's message of power and deliverance and freeing the souls of people who have all their lives been deprived of the fullness of God's word by Satan.

Our excitement being involved in something we felt was a major city wide outreach could not be extinguished or quenched. I was grateful that God would have found me worthy of such a great honor as to involve me at all. Both of us were like two raging fires. Nightly at the coffee house something exciting took place. Someone got saved, or baptized in the Holy Ghost, or healed. Usually on Sunday morning one of us was anxious to give a testimony at Church. We felt that everyone needed to know what the latest exciting thing was the Lord had done for us. I was so proud and happy every time something happened, I just could not keep it to myself. And mistakenly I really thought that everyone would share my enthusiasm. But I was wrong. One day we received an unexpected visit from our pastor. He was there to tell us that he would appreciate it if we would stop giving testimony in church, because we were making a lot of folks feel very uncomfortable. To say the least, I was shocked to realize that the folks at my church could care less about what God was doing in our lives.

All the tickets for the banquet sold within a couple of weeks. My neighbor who I had been witnessing to about the baptism of the Holy Ghost had sold a bunch of tickets at the First Baptist church where he was a member, but he did not buy any for himself. He told me that his pastor said that the experience was irrelevant, and might even be satanic, because the real baptism in the Holy Ghost had passed away with the disciples.

Finally the day came for which we had been laboring for about six weeks. We picked up the five speakers of the airlift team. We did not have a whole lot of time since they arrived in the late afternoon of the same day of the banquet. The next few days were going to be busy days for us, since we had to transport them for the next seven days to all the meetings we had booked for them.

After everyone had refreshed themselves at my friend's home, we had to leave for the banquet. All five of the speakers shared the time and gave their testimonies. After they all spoke, they began to call people out who wanted to be prayed for, for healing, salvation and the baptism of the Holy Ghost. About a dozen people from the First Baptist church were amongst the two hundred guests at the banquet. Three of the men who were elders, and one was a youth leader, decided that they knew that the baptism of the Holy Ghost was not for today and decided to challenge one of the speakers. When their turn came, the speaker who knew nothing of their plot to challenge him, just laid his hand on the shoulder of the first man to ask him what he wanted to be prayed for. But before the Baptist brother could say even one word, the Holy Ghost slew him on the floor flat on his back, where he started rolling around speaking in tongues. Then it was time for the other two brothers who were standing next to the one who got slain. It all happened so fast and took them completely by surprise. When the speaker asked the next brother what he wanted from the Lord, all he could say was, "Whatever the Lord wants to give me." The speaker laid hands on him and he and his friend who was still standing, both started to speak in tongues.

The meeting finished late and it was after two in the morning before we ever got to bed. The next day was Saturday and we did not have to get up early, but about eight o'clock we were still in bed when the door bell rang. I got up to see who it was, and when I opened the door the man who I had never met before introduced himself, and said he just wanted to thank me for having my neighbor sell him a ticket to the banquet. He said that he was the chief elder at the First Baptist church, and that he and two of his friends received the Baptism of the Holy Ghost at the meeting. He then explained to me about their plot. He went on to tell me how he was unable to sleep. Every time he tried to sleep, he said, a new burst of tongues came out of his mouth. Then he said his next stop was to thank my neighbor. I asked him to wait for me to get dressed so I could go with him. When I told Genny she also wanted to go.

When we arrived at my neighbor's house he and his wife invited us inside. My neighbor had told me before that this elder was very highly respected at the church. I was also told that he was quite wealthy, and practically paid for the construction of the church himself. When we walked in the house the elder started to tell my neighbor what happened to him, but before he could say much, he had fresh outburst of tongues. My neighbor and his wife were visibly shaken. I said to them, "Sit down. I'm here to thank you for selling him a ticket to the banquet. You remember how I have told you about the baptism in the Holy Ghost, and how you were scared that it might be from Satan? You see, now, your elder received the baptism from Jesus last night and you both could also have Jesus give the baptism of the Holy Spirit to you right this minute."

My neighbor at a loss for words said, "If God can give it to him, then I want it also." Genny and I laid hands on them and prayed for them and instantly the Lord baptized both of them also. How good is God? He is very good! Well, as we all know, once a person receives the promise of the Comforter, they might no longer be welcome at their church, especially when the church doesn't think it's from God. The pastor happened to be away that weekend and the youth leader who was one of the three who received the baptism of the Holy Ghost was appointed by the pastor to preach that Sunday. The youth leader stuttered. But that night of the banquet while he was lying on the floor, the Lord completely healed him. That morning, the church was amazed at the fluent way in which he was delivering his sermon. He shared with the church what had happened to him and some of the other men also were given a chance to share how the Lord baptized them in the Holy Ghost. By the time the Sunday service was over a few more members had received the Holy Ghost. And that was when their trouble started.

Jesus said, "For this purpose the Son of God was manifested, that He might destroy the works of the devil" (1 John 3:8). The devil is a deceiver and will do everything in his power to keep people from experiencing the fullness of God. But when the Light comes to people, new revelations begin to flow from into them through the Holy Spirit. That is why Satan is so fearful of people who have the Holy Spirit.

The Bible tells us how Jesus was the Light sent from God to invade the darkness. In other words we might conclude that Jesus, by baptizing people with the Holy Spirit, also delivers them from ignorance, allowing them to come into new revelation knowledge that flows from God. John the Baptist said this of Jesus: "That [He, Jesus] was the true Light which lighteth every man that cometh into the world" (John 1:9).

Some of the church members were highly indignant that people of their congregation would receive the Holy Ghost inside their Baptist church. So as soon as church got out they got on the phone and told the pastor that there was an emergency, and he had better get back soon before his whole church became Pentecostal. The pastor came back and instructed all the members who received the baptism to deny the experience and get back to normal. But the following Sunday, the wife of the wealthy Baptist elder, she had not received the baptism at that point, prayed and asked God to give to her what her husband had received. The Lord told her that during the Sunday morning service, when everyone knelt for prayer at the commencement of the service, which was customary at that church, that she should stand. She did as the Lord told her and the minute she got on her feet, before the prayer could even begin, the Lord baptized her in the Holy Ghost right there in the church. With the pastor watching, pandemonium broke loose as several more began to join in speaking in tongues. That meant the end of all the Holy rollers in that church. As soon as things quieted down the pastor took the opportunity to excommunicate all the members who had received the experience of the Holy Ghost.

Well, that was what they got for being happy in the Lord,

persecution. Remember these words of Jesus that came true for them:

> Think not that I come to send peace on earth: I came not to send peace, but a sword. For I am come to set a man at variance against his father, and a daughter against her mother, and the daughter in law against her mother in law. And a man's foes shall be they of his own household.
>
> Matthew 10:34–36

A Voice in the Stillness of the Night

They that trust in the Lord shall be as mount Zion, which can not be removed, but abideth forever.

Psalms 125:1

But as for Philip, an angel of the Lord said to him, Go over to the road that runs from Jerusalem through the Gaza desert, arriving around noon. So he did, and who should be coming down the road but the treasurer of Ethiopia, a eunuch of great authority under Candace the queen. He had gone to Jerusalem to worship at the temple, and was now returning in his chariot, reading aloud from the book of the prophet Isaiah. The Holy Spirit said to Philip, Go over and walk along beside the chariot! Philip ran and heard what he was reading and asked, Do you understand it? Of course not! the man replied. How can I when there is no one to instruct me? And he begged Philip to come up into the chariot and sit with him.

Acts 8:26–31 Living Bible

After my return from Europe in 1972, the Lord again reminded me that He wanted me to go to Bible college in America. One of the F.G.B.M.F.I. speakers who came over on the airlift, gave me the name of a Trinity Bible College, which was situated in Tulsa, Oklahoma. The Lord told me, "Write to Trinity, because that is where I want you to go." I told the Lord that was a very scary thought, and if He did not mind, then I would rather not go. I also told the Lord that I had no money saved, and did not know how I would support my family if I had to go.

But when after several weeks of praying about the situation, continually asking the Lord to please not let me go, and the Lord still impressing on me that I had to go, I sat down and wrote the college a letter.

While I was waiting for the reply, I started to get up out of bed at midnight every night to pray, still asking the Lord not to let me go to college. Then one day there came a letter from the college. I nervously opened it. It read, "We at Trinity are not setup to accommodate foreigners, but we suggest you try one of the colleges on the list we attached."

I was so happy that they did not want me. That night I prayed again and thanked the Lord that He changed His mind. I told the Lord that I was not preaching material anyway. I was just about to end my prayer and go back to bed when God spoke to me. How, I can not explain. I just knew that I knew as every child of God does. I knew something mysteriously supernatural happened and that the Lord had said to my spirit, "I want you to go to Trinity Bible College! But because you will question me I will give you a sign to confirm to you that I am calling you to preach the Gospel. Even though you are afraid, I assure you that I will be with you every step of the way. I will make a way for you to go, but you will have to stay in touch with me and not forget to talk to me every day about your progress. I know the college said that you can't come. Listen, this is what I want you to do.

Write and tell them not to be concerned, you will find your own way to get there without their help. Tell them God said you must go. Here is your sign: There is a man stranded on the mountain top. Get in your car and go and help him, and after you have helped him, you must lead him into salvation. If he accepts Jesus as his Lord and savior, let it be your sign that I am sending you to Trinity Bible College.

I grabbed my coat. I was mumbling to myself, "I know it was God who told me to go and get the man on the mountain, but what if it was just my imagination and what I thought I heard was not God at all. How will I find a stranded motorist on the mountain? It is after all one o'clock in the morning!"

The mountain top was about ten miles from where I lived. Once I got to the top of the mountain, I pulled over to the side of the road where there was an outlook. From where I sat in my car the view was breathtaking. I had never seen it at night. I could clearly see the coast line and the white waves as they broke under the full light of the moon. The city lights that lit up the sky above the city even further enhanced the beauty of the ocean view. I have always loved the ocean, which was one of the reasons I lived in this small town Somerset West. The town looked like it was cuddled into the side of the mountain.

I did not see a stranded motorist anywhere on the side of the road while I came up the mountain pass. I thought to myself, "I may as well go back home, I must have missed God." I knew I had to get home soon. Genny was working the night shift at the hospital, and in the morning at six o'clock, I would have to get up to get the children ready for school and drop them off on my way to work, and I needed to get some shut eye.

As I pulled my car around, and felt relieved that I did not find the man. I had hardly gone a half a mile when I passed a car on the side of the road. I knew the car was not there when I came up the mountain pass. I thought the car must have stopped there while I was sightseeing.

Then I wondered if that could have been the man. Then the Holy Spirit said to me, "That is your man. Go and get him." I slammed on the breaks and turned my car around and started back. As my lights lit up the scene in front of me, I saw a man sitting in the car. I stopped, and as I stopped the man got out of his car. I got out also and inquired what was wrong. The man said he had a flat tire and that his spare tire was also flat. I offered to take him to a service station if any were open, so we put his flat spare tire in my car.

As we started down the mountain, I asked the man, "Where are you going to?"

The man replied, "I am local, I live in town." He continued to tell me that he had been at a dance at the hotel on top of the mountain and was on his way home when he had a flat tire.

I then said to him, "Are you a Christian?"

"Not really." he said. "My mother, now she is a wonderful Christian."

I was trying to seize the best moment to tell the man why I was there to help him. I already realized the man probably wouldn't believe my story if I told him that God had told me to help him. I said to him, "You are very lucky because God loves you even if you are not a Christian as you said yourself."

Apparently, I struck a nerve. The man almost exploded next to me. "God love me?" he said. "Man, you must be kidding me. God does not love me. Do you know how bad things are going for me? Well, I will tell you." He continued without waiting for any reply from me.

"Tonight my best friend took my girl and went off with her in his car. It made me so mad I could kill him. That was when I got into my car and left also. Just as I pulled out of the parking lot at the hotel, I had a flat tire. I changed tires and put on my spare. Before I reached the highway, I had another flat tire. But lucky for me, my brother and I drive the same model car, and today I picked up his spare tire for him and still had it in my car trunk, so I put his tire on my car. But right there where you found me, I had my third flat tire, and you say God loves me. No! I tell you if there even is such a thing as a God, he does not love me or care about me. And that is not all." He continued, "On my job, my manager and I just don't get on together. Everything in my life is going the wrong way, so you see God does not love me."

After all of that outburst I did not quite know what to say to him, but by the time he had told me his sad trailblazer of mishaps and disillusionment, we had reached the town and started to circle the few gas stations we thought might still be open for service. But we could not find anyone still open and the clock was edging on to two o'clock. I said, "Well, what do you want to do now?"

The man said, "If you could take me by my mother's house to get a coat and take me back to my car, I would really appreciate it." We stopped by his mother's house and I was surprised to see the house ablaze with all the lights still on.

When an older lady came to the door, she did not look like she had gone to bed yet. I could see from where I sat and waited in my car that she was still fully dressed. When my stranger friend got back into the car, I remarked, "Does all of your family keep such late hours?"

"Well," he replied, "that lady is my mother. You see, I am thirty years old and she still worries about me. Every time I am out late like tonight, she stays up and waits for me. You see, my mother I suppose is a little like you. She thinks I am on my way to hell, and she stays up to pray for me, and she will stay up until

I get back home. Now tell me if that is not the craziest thing you have ever heard?"

"No." I replied. "I think she does it because she loves you. But there is someone who loves you even more than she does. His name is Jesus, and while you were out there changing those flat tires tonight, He spoke to me and said, 'Get into your car and go and help a man on the mountain that is in trouble.' God also said for me to tell you that tonight is your night to get saved. So you see, that is why I was there to help you tonight."

I could not see the man's face in the dark, but he was noticeably shook up. Almost screaming, he said, "Man! You are crazy! You surely don't expect me to believe that story you just told me is true. It can't be true, how can you even prove what you say is the truth?"

I replied, "I can't." Then the Holy Spirit said to me, "Show the man you are in your pajamas."

I said, "Tell me, how often have you seen someone driving down the road in their pajamas?" With my one hand I pulled my coat open so the man could see that I had my pajamas on. Without waiting for a reply from him, I continued, "Tonight while you were cursing your friend going off with your girlfriend, and were mad about your flat tires, I had already gone to bed and gotten up to pray, when the Lord said to me, 'Go find a man in trouble on the mountain.' And from what you tell me, your mother was probably also praying at the same time. Now you tell me, why would God tell me to go and get you if He did not love you? And what other possible reason could I have for driving you around? It is now after two in the morning and I need to get some sleep."

Neither the man nor I said another word until we reached his car. We took his still flat spare tire out of my car trunk. Then the man said to me with a tremor in his voice, "Sir, if Jesus loves me as much as you say He does, would you please pray with me and ask Him to help me change my life?" We knelt down on the gravel next to the man's car. I started to pray for him, and was still praying when the man pleadingly began to cry out to God for himself. That was the moment that I knew that man had made contact with his Savior for himself.

How good is God? He is very good!

It is my firm belief that when we accept Jesus Christ as our Savior, we are born into a new family-God's family-at that moment the Holy Spirit is given to me by Christ as my lifelong partner to teach me and guide me into my relationship with my Father, my God. If I pay attention to His voice, that still small voice on my inside where He, the Holy Spirit presides, He will instruct me into the God kind of wisdom. In that I will begin to do things, everyday things, the kind of things we all do every day, differently. I willingly yield myself to do what He tells me to do. Once I have accomplished the yielding of my will to Him, I will then begin to step into the promises Jesus gave us:

> But seek ye first the kingdom of God, and His righteousness; and all these things shall be added unto you. Take therefore no thought for tomorrow: For the morrow shall take thought for the things of itself, Sufficient is the day and the evil thereof.
>
> Matthew 6:33–34

Only God knows what tomorrow holds, and since He is willing to take responsibility for me, it would be absolutely foolishness on my part to not let Him. I now realize that He wants to share with me His irrefutable riches, His divine word to keep me healthy, His unfathomable wisdom to guide my life to be as successful as I willingly allow Him to make me into that new creature. You see, you and I are restricted and He is not. Why should I not trust Him and experience His Glory? God is the one who sent His only Son to redeem me from the curse of the law and made me an heir of the blessing covenant that He made with Abraham.

> Christ redeemed us from the curse of the law, being made a curse for us, for it is written, cursed is everyone that hangeth on a tree.
>
> Galatians 3:13

> That the blessings of Abraham might come on the Gentiles, through Jesus Christ; that we might receive the promise of the Spirit through faith.
>
> Galatians 3:14

I am then according to God's word no longer part of the sinful world who still falls under the curse, but I am now one of God's sons, led by His Spirit.

Once I got hold of a book by Dr. Oral Roberts, called *Seed Faith.* The reading of this book and the opening of the scriptures truly revolutionized my life. I was not a giver, but after reading seed faith, I said, "Okay, God, show me." I started by giving God 10% of the gross of my income. But one month later the Lord came to me and said, "Give me 20%." One month after that the Lord came back and said, "Now give me 30%."

Genny said to me, "How can I manage my housekeeping if you give all the money away?"

I said to her. "Did you run short last month?"

She said, "No."

I tested God and God was testing me. We went all the way up to giving 90% of my income going to the Lord and in some supernatural way, I was still able to pay all my bills. This is the time during which I began to receive double pay checks, something quite unheard of when you work for the government.

Why am I telling you about this? With God there are no limits. We limit ourselves through unbelief, or lack of teaching, or the understanding of God's precious promises.

God is also Our Father

For you did not receive the spirit of slavery to fall back into fear, but you have received the spirit of sonship. When we cry Abba Father! It is the Spirit Himself bearing witness with our spirit that we are the children of God, and if Children then heirs of God and fellow heirs with Christ. Provided we suffer with Him in order that we may also be glorified with Him!

Romans 8:15–17 RSV

Today we live in a society that has become indifferent. Somehow many of God's people have never experienced a real family bond. Many children who grew up in a single parent family only bonded with their moms. Still many children grow up not even having any parent to bond with period.

There is no doubt in my mind that these people find it particularly hard to understand what it really is like to have a loving and caring father. Thus they are incapable to grasp the powerful trust that develops through bonding. In the days of the Apostle Paul when the above scripture was written people could identify easier with the powerful analogy in comparing our heavenly Father with our parenting father. However, even though many have never experienced bonding, the Holy Spirit can help anyone who sincerely seeks after the truth to receive revelation knowledge to grasp the significance of this parallel. God is a good God, who only wants the very best for His children. He does not in any way love Christ anymore than He loves us. Here the Bible tells us that through Jesus we received equal treatment from our heavenly Father. God loves us just as much as He loves Jesus, His only begotten son.

In my interpretation of God's word, I understand that God will stand behind me as His child through thick and thin. When my children were small, I helped my wife with them when I was at home. I would bathe and feed them. I would play games with them and help them with their school assignments. It is my firm belief that a real man's kind of man is not ashamed to love and hold and take care of his children. Neither does he expect his wife to become a slave to his children because of some sick notion that raising one's own children and doing house chores is not a manly thing to do. I am very assured that my heavenly Father takes time out of His busy schedule to answer my insignificant questions and listen to my prayers.

After the mountain experience God gave me, I had finally come to the realization that God seriously wanted me to go to Trinity Bible College in the United States. I wrote back in reply of their letter in which they rejected my application, telling me that they were not set up to accommodate foreign students. I told them that God still wanted me to come and asked them to please go ahead and enroll me for the next semester.

The time had finally come for my lovely wife, Genny, who has always been so kind and supportive of my impromptu revelations, to begin to talk about our going to Bible college. Both of us realized that we had several obstacles to overcome before we could go to Bible college: Would the college accept me? Would they believe my letter, in which I said that God wanted me to come anyway? Where would I get enough money to finance such an undertaking? I did not even know how to estimate the cost, because I did not know at the time what I had to pay for college. I had no idea of the cost of living, renting a place to stay, etc., in America. Would I have to resign my position at the hospitals or would they grant me leave of absence? Would we take the children with us or find someone to keep them until we got back? What would we do with our house, rent it or sell it? Why me, God, why Bible college? I was happy until then. I was happy with my life. I went to church, and I witnessed. Wasn't that enough?

I had already told God that I had no desire to be a preacher. So in view of my personal opinion I thought it would be a total waste of time to send me to Bible college. But in all sincerity, I had the distinct feeling that God had different plans in store for me. He already had His mind made up that I was going to go to Bible college. "Well, I will go," I thought to myself, "just as long as God realized that there is no way I would ever get up in front of a big crowd to speak." No one knew my limitations any better than I did. Genny was not particularly overly thrilled with the idea either. Her biggest concern was the safety of our four children and what kind of an impact it would have on them.

Between the two of us we spent the next several weeks doing some very serious praying. If ever we needed the mind of Christ it was then. This particular morning I was on my way to work. I used to have to drive an hour or more to work every day depending on which hospital I was working at. The time alone in the car was my opportunity to worship and sing praises to the Lord. At times my communion with the Lord in the car could become quite intensive. There were times I could feel the presence of the Lord in such a powerful way that words could never describe it. That was such a morning in the car on my way to work when the

Lord spoke to me, and said, "Go and talk to the bank manager and ask him to loan you two thousand Rand" (the equivalent of $6,000 American dollars). In 1973 that was a lot of money.

The next day I went to see the bank manager whom I had never met before. After waiting a while to see him, I was ushered into his office. I was pointed to a seat and the door closed behind me as I sat down. The man on the other side had a hard stern face. "What can I do for you?" he wanted to know.

I replied, "I need a loan for two thousand Rand." He looked at me for a moment and asked, "What kind of collateral can you give me?"

I thought for a minute, not sure how to answer him, when he asked the next question,

"Do you own your own home? How much do you owe on your mortgage?" he asked.

"Yes, I do." I replied.

"How many years have you owned it?" he wanted to know next.

"About two or three years." I replied.

"Not good enough." he said. "What else do you have?"

"Nothing except a wife and four kids," I replied.

His decision was made. Without a blink he said, "Sorry, I can't help you. Your collateral is not sufficient."

I was not in a mood to argue with him. So, I stood up to leave. The man stretched his hand out to me for the first time to say goodbye. "What did you want the money for?" he asked, as if it would make any difference now after he already said no.

Indifferent to his question I said, "I am planning to go to Bible college," and started towards the door.

"Where is the Bible college you are going to?" he half shouted as I began walking out the door.

I half turned around to answer him. "It is Trinity Bible College in Tulsa, Oklahoma. It's in America," I added on just in case he did not know where Tulsa, Oklahoma, was.

His next words almost knocked me of my feet. "Come back here." he shouted. "Why did you not tell me that you want the money for Bible college in the first place? I also believe in God and I don't want to hinder His work. Come back and sit down." I came back into his office, sat down and he wrote me a check for two thousand Rand and said, just take this down to any teller, they will cash it for you.

After I got back into my car I thought to myself, "That was so easy, and probably only because God was involved. If I was on my own trying to get that loan, I would never have gotten it."

A few days passed before God gave me the next step. God said, "Go to your mortgage holder and ask him to freeze the mortgage on your house until you return from Bible college." Freeze my payments? Now I had never heard of anything like that before and wondered if the people at the mortgage company had heard about freezing one's mortgage payments.

The next day I was at the mortgage company. The Manager was very friendly until I asked him if he could freeze my house payments for two years. He looked at me kind of strange then said, "I don't think that it is impossible, but I would have to take your request to the next board meeting. You see I have never had a request to freeze someone's payments and I don't know that we can do it." He gave me a date to call him back. Two weeks later when I called him back, and he said, "No problem, your request was granted. Just give me the date you want us to start freezing your payments." I thought to myself, "God you are really incredible. I get to do things the bank did not even know they could do."

In the meantime I had also written to one of the F.G.B.M.F.I. brothers who was in Cape Town during the airlift. I wrote and asked him about the cost of living to give me some idea as to how much money I should bring with me. I felt that I had a lot of faith, but what if God forgot about me while I was over there? It was not that I did not trust God. No, I think it was more a fear that I myself might miss God's direction.

It took over a month before I received a reply. I eagerly opened the letter to see what the brother had to say. What I read made me kind of mad. He did not answer any of my questions. The letter simply said, "Brother Corrie, just get yourself over here. Don't worry about anything, God will take care of you. Call me the minute you arrive at the Tulsa Airport. Someone will come and get you."

"Now what help is that to me?" I asked Genny and added, "What he said in the letter I already knew. I knew that God would take care of me. But I still need money and common sense, don't I? The brother in America did not answer even one of my questions." Now I know what the brother meant was, "Don't worry, God will take care of all your needs." But my question was, "How?"

I know what Jesus says in Matthew 6:31–34. He tells us not to worry about what we will eat, or drink, Jesus continues and said that our heavenly Father knows that we need all these things. Like most people, I was accustomed to taking care of myself. I thought that God would have expected me to take care of myself. I did not really understand that I could ever be important enough for God to want to take care of me just for me. Today I fully realize that every person, no matter who they are, is all of equal importance to God. I mean that the heir, as long as he is a child, is no better than a slave, though he is owner of the estate, but he is under guardians and trustees until the date set by the Father. "Now I say, That the heir, as long as he is a child, differeth nothing from a servant, though he be lord of all" (Gal 4:1).

Do we act like we are slaves? Unable to enjoy our inheritance left to us in our Father's will? What can I benefit from my relationship with my heavenly Father? A question many believers could not answer. I know I could not have answered either up until that point in my life. I was going to find out real soon. I was also going to find out that to become a participant and co-heir with Christ required responsibilities I had never even considered before. Just being a church member was a lot easier.

Genny's and my relationship with our heavenly Father was taking us into a direction we could not have imagined. It had become time for me to approach my superiors and ask for two years of unpaid leave. It was easier than I thought. The new kitchen we designed was pumping out ten to fifteen thousand meals a day with no problem. Everything was operating smoothly. When the day came for me to ask my bosses for a couple of years off to go to Bible college, they agreed, and said I could get the time off. "But," they said, I had to train someone to replace me. They said I could handpick whomever I wanted and teach that person everything I knew. Well, I was not going to worry about who to pick. I felt sure the Lord would direct me and He did. Everything was now falling into place.

However, two of our concerns remained unanswered. First, why did the Lord want me to go to Bible college? Was it just a test of obedience, or was God rearranging my life for me? I continued to struggle with that. Second, we still did not know where or with whom to leave the children.

Both Genny and I understood God's instructions that we should not take the children with us. That was very hard for both Genny and me. Genny accepted the word the Lord gave us on the children and tried all she could to find peace about it. But in the end she suffered a nervous breakdown. A pastor friend and I prayed for two weeks around the clock, standing in the battle with her. She was totally unaware of anyone's presence around her. She did not answer any questions or acknowledge anyone's presence. For two weeks she stayed in bed and had no communication with anyone. She did not eat or acknowledge anyone talking to her. After two weeks she came out of it and resumed her life as if nothing ever happened. But during that time God apparently gave her total peace. She had overcome her fear and knew without a shadow of a doubt that God would and could take care of her children while she was at Bible college.

After Genny's episode, I finally came to the realization that God was not just testing my obedience. I was going to go to Bible college and that was all there was to it. The days were flying by and two weeks before we had to leave for the States, we still had nowhere and no one to leave our children with. Then one day I had the most unexpected phone call.

My brother, who was nine years younger than me, lived a life just the opposite to mine. He was a very successful businessman and he and his wife had no children of their own. He never went to church and lived in the fast lane. His wife was no different, and because I would get on them and remind them that God was watching them, I caused her to hate me. She once said that she wished that somehow they could fasten me to a satellite and leave me up in space so she would not ever have to see me again.

That evening I was sitting in the living room listening to the news on the radio, since in 1973 there was no television in South Africa yet. When the phone rang, I picked it up. To my utmost surprise it was Boet, my brother. "We are coming to Cape Town on business tomorrow," he informed me. "We want to come by and see you for a few minutes if that is okay."

I said, "Sure. We will be to happy to see you." Not exactly the truth, but I always tried to make him feel welcome. In Paul's letter to the Thessalonians he tells us this, "See that none renders evil for evil unto any man; but ever follow that which is good, both among yourself and to all men" (1 Thessalonians 5:15).

So even though a visit from my brother was not exactly something I was going to look forward to, I still wanted to receive him in a Christ-like manner.

About seven o'clock that next evening a car pulled up in front of the house and I met Boet and his wife, Valery, at the front door. I welcomed them and asked them inside. My children were usually happier than me to see their uncle, who always brought them some kind of small gifts. After all the hugs and kisses were over the children went to bed.

Back in the living room we all got settled down to visit. I had this strange feeling that there was more to this visit than we knew. As soon as they sat down I said, "What brings you to Cape Town? I did not know that your company conducted business out here."

He looked at me for a minute before his wife broke the silence. She said, "Well, yes, you are right, his company does not conduct any business in Cape Town. This trip was for my benefit. Two weeks ago God saved me in a church service. It was so powerful what happened to me, I don't have the words to describe it. When Jesus washed away my sins, He also washed away all the hatred I had for you. Then Jesus told me that I had to come to you in person to tell you I am sorry and ask your forgiveness."

Involuntary tears welled up in my eyes; I was happy for her that she now knew the same Jesus I knew. It always amazes me how the Holy Spirit can take a totally dull evening and change it into a prayer meeting at the flip of a penny. Only God can send someone a thousand miles to go and ask forgiveness in person. With the sweet presence of the Holy Spirit in the room, overwhelming joy instantly flooded my heart and in seconds Valery,

Genny and I were all shedding tears of joy with Valery. What else was there to do but to be happy with her and praise the Lord? God had taken her heart of stone and hate and replaced it with love and compassion. "And to know the love of Christ, which passeth knowledge, that ye might be filled with all the fullness of God" (Ephesians 3:19).

God had filled Valery with Himself and I had no doubt about it. After we settled down again they wanted to know what we had been doing. Since because of our past differences we had little to say to each other before now, they had no idea that God had been using Genny and me. Neither did they know that we had plans to go to Bible college. We just started to tell them a little about what God had been doing in our lives. But before I could even tell them we were soon leaving for Bible college, Valery said she had something else that she had to tell us. Without waiting for approval from anyone to speak Valery interrupted and said, "God told me that there was something very important that I had to do for Him and for you. But I have no idea what it is. God said that he would show me what it was while I was down here."

Genny and I looked at one another not sure what she was talking about. What was very evident was the glow on Valery's face and her new found joy in Jesus. After her interruption, we continued to tell them what God had been doing in our lives. When I came to share how the Lord was directing us to go to Bible school, Valery interrupted again, "And what are you going to do with the children?" She wanted to know.

"Well," I said, "Genny and I have been waiting on the Lord to tell us what we should do with the children. He said He would show us when the time came. Thus far He has not shown us."

"That must be it!" Valery shouted excitedly. "That must be what God wants me to do! He wants me to take care of your children while you are at Bible college." My mind at first could not comprehend the idea of Valery taking care of the children and neither could Genny's. This woman that has been so hostile for so long, coming to us out of the blue, confessing salvation, and now she offers to take our children in her care? This seemed too convenient, even suspicious.

Valery, sensing our uneasiness, simply said, "Think about it over night. We are also tired, after all, we drove a thousand miles to get here. I suggest Boet and I get a room and come back to talk to you in the morning. In the meantime you can pray about our offer and I will also pray about it." That sounded fair to me and I agreed. We said good bye and after they left, Genny and I sat for a long time talking about what just happened. Was that possible that God had saved Valery out of a life of sin and completely changed her life around, just in time to take care of our kids while we would be at Bible college? What if after a few months she decided that what she felt about what God was asking her to do was a mistake and the children became so burdensome to her she wanted to quit? Then what would we do twelve thousand miles on the other side of the world? After a long talk, Genny and I spent time praying about what we should do, asking God to confirm to us if Valery's offer was indeed from Him. The scripture God gave us said this:

> For every one who asks receives, and he who seeks finds, and to him who knocks it will be opened. Or what man of you, if his son asks him for bread, will give him a stone? Or if he asks for a fish, will give him a serpent? If ye then who are evil, know how to give good gifts to your children, How much more will your Father who is in heaven give good things to those who ask Him!
>
> Matthew 7:8–11 RSV

The next morning after we got up Genny and I both felt that we had peace about the situation. We both felt that our heavenly Father would not set up a trap for us. It was hard for me to believe that the same person who for years was my biggest enemy now felt that God had commissioned her to care for our children while we're at Bible college. But Jesus said, I am to trust my Father in heaven. Genny and I had been praying for many months and, as it was, we only had two more weeks before we had to leave. The more we talked about it, the more the whole situation was taking on the characteristics of an out and out miracle. Especially since neither Boet nor Valery had any idea that we were even praying, asking God to give us a place for the children. A lot of sudden surprises, but then in God's secret kingdom, I have learned that surprises are to be expected. In fact, in God's secret kingdom surprises could be considered normal. I even started to feel so proud. Just to think my heavenly Father did that all for me. I realized that my Father had developed a working relationship with Genny and me that was continuing to grow. Now all I had to do was to continue to believe. That also meant that I should never doubt my Father, and really listen for His replies when I talked to Him in prayer. "For therein is the righteousness of God revealed from faith to faith: as it is written the just shall live by faith" (Romans 1:17).

Living in the Lord every day requires a certain amount of faith. Jesus said about answering our prayers that we have to believe that our heavenly Father is going to give us what is right. I also have to believe that He won't allow me to walk into a trap. So with those thoughts in mind, Genny and I accepted Valery's offer to take in our children. She promised over and over that she was going to take care of them as unto the Lord.

All the arrangements were falling right into place. Genny would take the children by train to Boet and Valery in Durban, stay a few days to get them enrolled into school and when they all settled in she would fly up to Johannesburg, where we would catch our flight together to New York.

But the night before Genny was to leave with the children, she had a horrible dream. Neither of us usually placed too much stock into dreams. However, the Lord had spoken to Genny a few times through a dream. When Boet described to us where they lived, he said that his house was only a stone's throw from the beach in Durban. Since we had never been to his house, we did not really know just how far from the beach he lived. Genny in her dream saw that she and the children were at Boet's house. The house was practically on the water front. There was a fence around the house, but the gate was not locked, and in her dream, Genny saw the twins, who were about seven years old at the time, just walk out the gate. Next, she saw them in the water, and without any warning, a large wave washed up on the beach and both the boys were swept into the ocean in the backwash. By the time she was able to get to them, they had both drowned and their lifeless little bodies were lying washed up on the beach sand. She woke up in a cold sweat. Her first words to me after she woke me up was, "You're going to have to go to Bible college by yourself, because something terrible is going to happen to the twins if we leave them with Valery."

This was not a dream from God, but from Satan. Both God and Satan communicate to us through dreams. Remember, we are always in the center of the battle field and this battle is not ours, it is a battle between *Two Invisible Kingdoms*. The price is for winning human beings. That is why God was willing to give His only Son as a sacrificial price to buy back my redemption, or freedom. To Satan we become slaves—slaves of sex, or fear, depression, hopelessness, drugs, money, anger, un-forgiveness, sports, television, hobbies, good works-whatever you can think of that is addictive, Satan will make you a slave to that thing, even preaching or religion. God, on the other hand, paid the highest price that could ever be paid to give me back my freedom.

She anxiously shared her dream with me. Genny felt that there was a possibility that the dream came to her from God as a warning. We sat and talked about her dream for a while. I felt that the Holy Spirit was saying to me, "Your children could get run over tomorrow when they cross the street on their way to school, if their angels were not there to protect them. So then, why would God save Valery and send her a thousand miles to offer to take care of your children, if God was not in the business of giving good gifts to His children? After all, are you not His Child? And did you not ask Him for this gift? If you believe then that God is your Father, you have nothing to be concerned about."

After weighing all the odds we decided that the dream was not from God after all and felt that it was sent as a deception from Satan. The age old trick, Satan's question, the one he asked Eve in the garden of Eden, "Did God say?" In this instance, "Can you trust God?" Genny and I decided right there and then that Satan had no part in our relationship with God and we would not afford him the joy of shipwrecking the miracle God gave us. Building is God's business and breaking down is all Satan is good at.

It came to two days before I was flying out to meet Genny in Johannesburg. She was already at Boet and Valery's. Genny and Valery went together to enroll the children in their new schools. Genny said they were all happy and everything looked like it was going to work out just right. The house in her dreams that sat on the beach? Well, that was just another distraction from the enemy to try and derail us. I was glad we had enough faith that day and did not believe the dream from the enemy. The house was near the ocean all right. But there ran an interstate highway between the house and the beach. There was no way to take a short cut to the beach by crossing the highway either; the interstate was fenced on both sides and the beach was over mile away. It is amazing that Satan can never get his facts together. However, it is equally amazing that many of God's precious children are robbed every day by Satan who still trips up many of God's precious children by using the same old ploy he used with Eve, "Did God say?"

Walking with God had become very exciting for both Genny and me. When one understands the rules of God's kingdom, and the principles of faith, it becomes easier to walk with and to trust God, understanding that God is a builder of good things and good relationships. On the other hand Satan is a destroyer of good things and wrecks relationships. I would suggest that every child of God read Matthew five, six and seven over and over and over, until the Holy Spirit fully reveals to you the power of the words of Jesus. It is the rules of the new covenant as implemented by Jesus himself. Apply it to your everyday life. Read those chapters in as many different Bible translations as you can lay your hands on. And always keep in mind that practice makes perfect. The more one follows the directions Jesus gave us, the better one will begin to comprehend why God sent His Son to pay the penalty of our sins and redeem us from the curse. God only wants one thing for us as His children, and that one thing is to restore our joy. It is the joy Satan stole from Eve in the garden and Satan still displaces the joy of many of God's children even today. Jesus told us that He was going to leave His joy with us before returning to His Father's house.

> If you keep my commandments, and you will abide in my love, just as I have kept my Fathers commandments and

abide in His love. These things I have spoken to you, that my joy may be in you, and that your joy may be full.

John 15:10–11 RSV

God wants us to have joy. But the only way we can realize His joy is to follow the directions given to us in the "Operations Manual," the Word of God.

I was really happy. Everything was falling into place. I was even happier that there was absolutely nothing that could happen to upset our plans. I had our plane tickets and I had my money. Perhaps not enough, but the brother in Tulsa that wrote to me said in his letter: "Just come and trust God, He will take care of you." Well, with the money I had I felt that I had enough faith to trust God for the rest. Especially having experienced all the interaction from God that I experienced in the past year. Yes! I believe that right then I had enough faith to move any mountain. I had only two more days and I would be on my way.

I was still savoring my thoughts when the door bell rang. I wondered who it could be, perhaps the couple who was going to rent the house from me while I was at Bible college. I got up and opened the door. It was Gerry, an evangelist I had met a few years ago. I had no idea why he would be visiting me, since he had never visited me before. After we had greeted and sat down in the lounge I asked him what he was up to.

"Getting ready to go to the United States," was his reply. "And this time I am taking the whole family with me," he continued. "The Lord told me that this time I could take my family with me." Gerry made regular trips to the United States by himself to raise money for missions in South Africa. After telling me his plans, he then inquired as to how we were doing and I gave him an update on us. Next we compared the dates we were going to leave. He was leaving the day after me.

I said, "Well, I suppose you have your tickets and you are all excited about leaving?"

He said, "Yes, we are excited, but we don't have our tickets yet, because I am short 2,000 Rand [$6000 U S dollars]. But the Lord said I will have the money in time to get my tickets." Then he said, "You probably wonder why I came to see you? When I prayed this morning the Lord told me I had to come and see you." Just about then I felt a sick feeling coming all over my stomach. I asked him if he would like something to drink and went to the kitchen to get it.

As soon as I was by myself I said, "Lord please tell me what is going on here. Why is he at my house?" I could feel my knees getting weak under me and that overwhelming bad feeling on my stomach when the Lord said to me, "Do you have your tickets paid for?" I said, "Yes, Lord, my tickets are paid for." Then the Lord said, "Give Gerry the money he needs for his tickets. I will take care of you when you get to America." Instead of pouring the drinks, I pulled up a chair at the kitchen table. I suddenly felt too weak to stand on my feet and I had to sit down. I said, "You know, Lord, when I get to New York, the customs officers are going to ask me to declare how much money I am entering the country with. If I tell them all I have is two hundred dollars, they will send me back home on the first available flight." After taking a breather, the Holy Spirit said to me, "Just have faith. What God has for you is more than you have."

The words of Jesus where he was instructing His disciples began to flash like neon lights in my mind:

Don't take any money with you; Don't even carry a duffel

> bag with extra clothes and shoes, or even a walking stick; for those you help should feed and take care of you.
>
> Matthew 10:9–10 TLB

> But seek first the kingdom and his righteousness, and all these things shall be yours as well. Therefore do not be anxious, for tomorrow will be anxious for itself. Let the days own trouble be sufficient for the day.
>
> Matthew 6:33–34 RSV

After I recovered from the shock of having to pay the airline tickets for the evangelist, I poured Gerry and myself each a drink. I felt I could really use something cold to swallow down all that anxiety. God was teaching me as I obeyed Him, one step at a time. I was learning things in this covenant walk with the Lord that were never taught in my church. Sadly most churches don't teach you this covenant stuff. I understood what God was saying to me. I realized that it was God who told me to go to Bible college. It was also God who had directed my every step to even have gotten to that point ready to depart for Bible college. It was God who saved Valery to take care of my four lovely children whom I love so much. Now God was saying to me again, "If I could take care of you this far, just continue to trust me and I will take care of you the rest of the way." I certainly did not want to contaminate this relationship between me and God with doubt and I certainly did not want Satan to have the satisfaction that he was able to derail me by instilling fear into my mind. I went back to the living room and took Gerry his drink. I knew I had no choice, not if I wanted to stay in God's economy.

After I sat down, I said, "Gerry, can you meet me tomorrow

around noon at my office and I will give you the money for your tickets." The biggest smile I had ever seen came across Gerry's face. He did not thank me for helping him. He simply said, "I knew today was the day God would give me my money. I just had to obey Him."

God was allowing me to have fellowship with some of His covenant children. Until now my fellowship in the church did not really include believers who understood the covenant. I did not fully comprehend the power and the joy of walking with God in the new covenant either at that point in my life, but God was teaching me; all I had to do was to be obedient and allow Him to direct me every day.

The African tribes really understand covenants better than anyone I know. Once they had cut a blood covenant nothing could break it, except death. Once two people had entered into a blood covenant, usually done by cutting the wrists of both parties, the blood from both parties is then mixed with wine and they both drink it. Each one then also gives the other one a gift. Once this formality is completed only death can break that covenant. If one breaks such a covenant, one's own family will turn against one and demand one's punishment which will be that person's death.

Paul clarifies the power of the covenant for us in the book of Hebrews. Because the Old Covenant sacrifices could not remit one's sin, but the blood of Christ does:

> Therefore He is the mediator of a new covenant, so that those who are called may receive the promised inheritance, since a death had occurred which redeems them from the transgressions under the first covenant. For where a will is involved, the death of those who made it must be estab-

> lished. For a will takes effect only at death, since it is not in force as long as the one who made it is still alive. Hence even the first covenant was not ratified without blood.
>
> Hebrews 9:15–18 RSV

I understand that my *Father* accepted me as a co-heir with Christ Jesus. Because His first Son Jesus, at His death made a covenant with the apostles to induct every person into the God family, everyone who would accept His sacrifice as the only begotten Son of God. If you have not yet made a choice between the *Two Invisible Kingdoms,* I urge you now to do so. You are already serving one of them, either by choice-the Son of God, who allows us to choose-or Satan, who usurps, taking by force, believing he is justified to have you.

Now I am also God's son with access directly to my heavenly Father. I even carry the name of my new heavenly family.

> For this reason I bow my knees before the Father, from whom every family in heaven and on earth is named, that according to the riches of His glory, he may grant you to be strengthened with might through His Spirit in the inner man, and that Christ may dwell in your hearts through faith; that you, being rooted and grounded in love, may have power to comprehend with all the saints what is the breadth and the length and height and depth, and to know the love of Christ which surpasses knowledge, that you may be filled with all the fullness of God.
>
> Ephesians 3:14–19 RSV

Miracles from Heaven

In that day you will ask nothing of me. Truly, truly, I say to you, if you ask anything of the Father, He will give it to you in my name. Hitherto you have asked nothing in my name; ask, and you will receive, that your joy may be full.

John 16:23–24 RSV

And in praying do not heap up empty phrases as the gentiles do; for they think that they will be heard for their many words. Do not be like them, for your Father knows what you need before you ask Him. Pray like this:

Our Father who art in heaven, Hallowed be thy name.

Thy kingdom come, Thy will be done,

On earth as it is in heaven.

Give us this day our daily bread; And forgive our debts,

As we also have forgiven our debtors; And lead us not into temptation,

But deliver us from evil.

Matthew 6:5, 8–13

Genny and I arrived at New York airport. We were both tired. Over twenty hours stuck in a seat on a plane had certain disadvantages. However, we were eager to reach Tulsa, which was our final destination. Once we were out of the plane and had time to stretch our legs, we both felt better and ready for the remainder of our journey.

We followed the signs that said, "Customs for non residents of the United States." That was us, non residents. Once we arrived at the customs, there was what looked to me like thousands of people lined up in about twenty or more lines. I had never seen such a big airport, and the people looked like every nationality on earth was represented. Now the waiting started, and waiting had never been one of my characteristically strong points.

I looked for an official to speak to and spotted a lady on my far left. I walked up to her and asked, "How long will it take to get through customs?"

Instead of answering my question, she asked me, "What time is your connecting flight?"

I replied, "In two hours."

To which she simply said, "You'll make it," then turned her attention to someone else. I walked back to my line where Genny was standing and watched what I could see at the counters. Trying to peep over all kinds of heads, I saw some people's luggage got dumped out on the counter and shuffled off to the end of the counter while others simply got passed over. Still others got pulled over to the side and escorted to some offices. I wondered if those who got escorted did not have enough money, like me. I had no idea what to expect when it would be finally my turn. And all that hair! All the colors of the rainbow. Some thick, some thin, some nice, some greasy. How in the world does God get to keep count of all that hair? It seemed so unnecessary to count everyone's hair. Why does God want to keep a accurate count of our hair? Imagine the complicated accounting system God must have in place to count all those heads of hair. But then on the other hand, I wondered why God would pick little old me, and tell me to go to Bible college? Truly amazing! My heavenly Father is truly amazing!

With all the commotion going on, one wondered if the custom officials themselves knew what they were doing. I wanted to say a short prayer to remind the Lord that I only had two hundred dollars, since He had me give away all my money. But the Holy Spirit reminded me that it was unnecessary, God already knew that, because He was the one who told me to do it. "If you want to *please* God, or say anything to Him," the Holy Spirit said to me, "then speak His word, and confess that you know that God will supply all your needs according to His riches in Glory." So, I confessed the scripture the Holy Spirit reminded me to say.

We had been in the line for over an hour. I could see we wouldn't make it in time. An official in a uniform walked up to us, pointed at our luggage and asked, "Is that yours?"

"Yes," I said, not knowing what to expect.

"Follow me," he said and started to walk, grabbing one of our suitcases. We followed him and I tried to catch up with him.

"Where are we going?" I asked.

He replied, "Over to that counter to process your paper work."

"What about the luggage search?" I asked.

"Don't worry about that. We are backed up and we don't have time to search everyone's luggage," he replied. We arrived at the counter. The official stretched out his hand towards me and I handed him our paper work. He briefly glanced over it, stamped it and in about five minutes we were on our way. I breathed a sigh of relief, glad that the customs ordeal was behind us. Glad that they never asked me how much money I had.

We boarded our flight to Tulsa and for the longest time my thoughts were with my four children back in South Africa. I knew that they did not understand why Mommy and Daddy had left them behind. The truth was, neither did Mommy and Daddy. Leaving them behind was the hardest thing either one of us had to do thus far. But God very distinctly said, "Leave your children behind. I will give you someone to take care of them." And God did. He fulfilled His part of the deal; my part was to obey. As two disciples of Jesus, neither one of us had a choice but to obey. After Jesus baptized me first and later Genny with the Holy Ghost, we had been so happy and running over with joy, walking around with a silly grin all the time.

When my Lord and Savior gave His Life to save me from the burden of sin and imputed to me, *His righteousness,* there was nothing He could have asked that we would not have done. It is by faith in His atonement that God imputed to me the righteousness of Christ and made me a co-heir with Christ. I could never have earned His righteousness. The only way in which I could become righteous was to believe and by accepting Jesus as my Savior. That was so easy.

No one was with me the day I accepted Jesus. I was by myself on the beach. Despondent with the way my life was going. I just sat there and said to myself, "Today I am asking Christ to take control of my life." I asked Jesus to take over my life, and He did. He removed all my sin and guilt and actually covered me with His righteousness. Now when my heavenly Father looks at me, He does not see my sin or my short comings any more. All my Father sees is the *righteousness of Christ,* that has covered all of my past, present and future faults.

> Therefore, since we are justified by faith, we have peace with God through our Lord Jesus Christ. Through him we have obtained access to His grace in which we stand, and we rejoice in our hope of sharing the glory of God. More than that, we rejoice in our sufferings, knowing that suffering produces endurance, and endurance produces character, and character produces hope, and hope does not disappoint us, because God's love has been poured into our hearts through the Holy Spirit which has been given us.
>
> Romans 5:1–5 RSV

I had wondered for the longest time what kinds of suffering the Lord would introduce me to. Now I know, leaving behind my children for Bible College was the hardest thing I have ever had to do. But by faith, I was able to do that and gladly. Since I am justified by faith and not by works, I now want to follow my Savior where ever He leads me to go. The day I accepted the fact that I had become a co-heir of God through Jesus Christ, I also realized that I became a partaker of His sufferings. Finis Jennings Dake says this, "We have grace to endure trials without sustaining loss or deterioration. We are silver and gold when refined." Thus I have the assurance in me by the Holy Spirit that God will take care of my children and even they will not sustain any permanent damage because of this temporary separation from their parents. To us right then it was a suffering.

After all did Jesus not say that He required His followers to leave *children* behind? "He that loveth father and mother more than me: and he that loveth son and daughter more than me is not worthy of me" (Matthew 10:37).

Many of Christ's disciples went as far as to give their lives. Think of those gospel heroes who burned at the stake for the sake of the gospel like John Wyclif and William Tyndale. Think of the courage Martin Luther had to come against the Pope and the entire religious establishment of his day, when he on October 31, 1517 nailed his ninety five theses to the door of the university chapel in Wittenberg, Germany. Nothing could stop him. He was determined to bring the love of Jesus his savior to the lost of his generation.

I took Genny's hand in mine and together we prayed and asked God to let our children feel our love for them. The captain's voice just about then came over the intercom to fasten our seat belts as we were getting ready to land at Tulsa's international airport.

I did not know who to look for at the airport. We were standing waiting for our luggage to show up on the conveyor belt when I heard someone beside me say, "Are you Corrie and Genny from South Africa?"

I looked around and saw a skinny young man standing there, looking at me. I replied, "Yes, that's us."

He stretched out his hand to greet us and introduced himself as Dale Barber. "I am Ollie Barber's son, he sent me to come and get you." By the time we introduced ourselves, our luggage had shown up. Together with Dale's help we carried the luggage to where he had his car parked. It only took about fifteen minutes to reach Ollie's house. We had met Ollie before. Ollie was one of the five people on the F.G.B.M.F.I. airlift to South Africa. In fact, Ollie was one of the two brothers who stayed at my house. Ollie was also the one who said, "Just get yourself over here. God will take care of you."

It felt really good to see one familiar face. Lucy, Ollie's wife, wanted to serve some refreshments. She mentioned ice tea. I had never heard of ice tea, thought it revolting, and declined her offer and settled for a glass of water. Where I came from tea was served hot with milk and sugar. It did not take me long to realize that I was in a totally different culture. My glass of water was filled with ice. "What was wrong with these people?" I thought to myself. "Ice in the water?" Not wanting to appear ungrateful, I drank the water with the ice.

We chatted for a while, and we shared how the Lord had inspired us to come to Bible College. I also told Ollie how the Holy Spirit had caused such a rumpus in the First Baptist church near us, that the church had split. Nothing the pastor did could stop those who were baptized in the Holy Ghost from spreading their new found joy in desperation to save some in his church from experiencing the same joy. The pastor gave the ones who had the joy the left foot of fellowship, including the elder who had built the church. But God was blessing their new fellowship and they continued to witness.

After a while Ollie told me that he and Lucy had something they wanted to show us. "But first," Ollie said, "tell me if you have already arranged accommodations for yourself?"

I felt somewhat embarrassed to tell him I had no money to make any arrangements with. But instead I just said, "No, but I would appreciate your helping me to find something." He and Lucy then took us about thirty minutes out of town to a trailer park and showed us a travel trailer. Ollie said a few months ago the Lord told him to buy the trailer for which he had no need and have it ready when we got to the States. I said, "How much will this cost us?"

"Not a thing," Ollie replied. "I am doing it for the Lord, and you and Genny can live here rent free for the duration of your Bible College. We will pay the lot rental and utilities, so you don't have to worry about a thing."

I felt a lump forming in my throat. What was God doing to us? He already had this trailer secured and all the arrangements in place for my accommodation, rent free, and all the utilities taken care off. "Come inside and see if you like it," Lucy said, interrupting my thoughts. Genny and I stepped inside. It was beautiful.

"I love it," Genny assured Lucy.

"I also love it," I said. "And God told you to do it for us?" I asked.

"Yes!" Ollie said. "Open the cupboards." I started to open the cupboard doors. Every inch of space was full of food stuff. I opened refrigerator; that too was full of food. Ollie said, "Look what is on that table." I looked; it was full of College books, Bible dictionary, encyclopedia etc. Ollie said "Those are all the books you will need for the College."

I could feel that the tears were going to flow just about any second. I had to brace myself to hold them back. My Father left nothing out. He had taken care of all my needs. Even if I had not given all my money to that Evangelist and still had it, I could not possibly have provided all this. I whispered softly, "Thank you, Jesus. How could I have known? Is that why your word says, 'The just shall live by faith?' Is this what it means to become a covenant son of God, that our heavenly Father takes on our responsibilities? *Wow!*" I decided that it was time for me to share with Ollie and Lucy how the Lord had asked me to give my money to the Evangelist. Now I also had a better understanding of the body of Christ.

> "For as we have many members in one body, and all members have not the same office: So, being many, are one body in Christ, and every one members of another" (Romans 12:4–5).

It's so amazing that I could be a hand of Christ in South Africa, giving a servant of God a helping hand. At the same time someone else who also became a hand of the body of Christ twelve thousand miles away started to give a helping hand to me by providing that trailer. The members in the church where Ollie was a member also were part of this body, and they were the ones who supplied the food stuff. Ollie said that the church was going to continue to supply the food stuff; just let him know when we needed something. So every time we obeyed the Holy Spirit, who is the brain part of our body of Christ, so to speak, He, the Holy Spirit, coordinated all these different parts into a combined effort. And so the body is flawlessly synchronized, working together to build God's kingdom. How wonderful to be a part of this, His body.

How wonderful not to be alone and to know that even here in a foreign country, I am still part of the body. I did not have to try and justify my need, or beg or plead. God just took care of it through His body. Right now I had so much confidence. I also felt so much love. To think that my heavenly Father loved me that much. Nothing that ever happens can take away the confidence and sonship one feels when one realizes that, "Yes! Everything is working exactly as Jesus said it would!"

The First Day of College

As for these four children, God gave them knowledge and skills in all learning and wisdom, and Daniel had understanding in all wisdom and dreams.

Daniel 1:17

We were escorted to the opening service of the college. Some of the students attending had their families with them for this service. Part of the calendar of events for the evening was to introduce each new student who in turn had to say where they were from. When it came to our turn to be recognized, they said that they now wanted to introduce the couple from South Africa. Genny and I were sitting in the front row. We stood to our feet and everyone in the hall had turned around and was looking for a black couple to come in the door, until they realized we were already standing.

There were students from everywhere, with every kind of background. We had a couple of ex prisoners, a pastor, a medical doctor, and someone who was in political science; people who owned businesses and some who did not really know why they were there. Everyone, however, was there for the same reason: They all said God told them to come.

It did not take us long to make friends. A few of the students had rented a trailer in the same park where we were staying. About three months into the school some of the students were getting ready to drop out. But the Lord told Genny and I to take care of them and help them.

God was good to Genny and me. We were making straight A's. The Lord just opened His word to us every day. The president of the college, Dr. Charles Duncome, daily taught one of our classes. Every time he taught, he would bring the subject to a spiritual closing. We found that he had developed a real sensitivity awareness to the Holy Spirit. Dr. Duncome's sensitivity to the Holy Spirit had a definite impact on Genny and myself, which later showed up in our ministry.

I thought that God and I had an agreement that I would go to Bible college and when college was over, I would go back to my job. But for some reason the Lord forgot to tell that to Ollie. So to my surprise one day Ollie said to me, "We have booked you as the main speaker for our F.G.B.M.F.I. men's retreat in two weeks."

I said, "Ollie, I don't want to sound ungrateful, but the Lord and I have agreed that I will not have to speak anywhere. You see, I am not a public speaker, and I will just embarrass you. Sorry!"

"Not so fast," Ollie came back at me. "That was not what the Lord told me. I think you better go and pray about it."

"No need to pray about this, Ollie," I said. "When God told me to come to Bible college, I told Him then that I was no preacher. I came with the understanding that when college was over, I could return to my job."

"That," Ollie replied, "was not what the Lord told me. He told me to book you as our speaker and the brochures have already been printed and distributed. One other thing, if you want to know the truth, I also questioned the Lord about having you to speak. I already knew that you were not a public speaker and I don't want to be embarrassed either. I told the Lord that this retreat would have too many good men of God, which would include corporate business men, pastors of big churches, as well as chapter presidents, to have a novice like you speak. But I could not change His mind. God insisted that you were His choice. So I suggest you go home, and talk to the Lord about it. And one more thing, you better be good for at least forty minutes."

I left Ollie, very upset about this latest development. More than anyone, surely God knew how nervous I was to speak in front of a large group. I did not mind testifying in church; that I could handle. I could even handle the coffee house we had. I could handle witnessing one on one. But here in the United States of all places and that before pastors and business men. "Please, God" I said, "don't do this to me! I will not be able to do it!"

People were already, as it were, constantly correcting my speech. English was my second language; my mother tongue was Afrikaans. I could even speak some tribal languages. But here in the States people were not even speaking the king's English as I knew it. They were compromising English. "Butchering the language" is what Dr. Duncome used to say, to the extent that my English teacher would roll over in her grave if she had to hear it. But, this was America.

But all the praying in the world did not change the situation. So I decided to change my prayer, and asked God to help me through this ordeal. Up until then I did not even know that I had a testimony. One day I got myself a piece of paper and started to write down all the things I could remember that God had done for me. I read what I had written, and it only took me ten minutes. I tried to think of some more testimony to add on; little by little I was getting there. After a couple of days I was up to twenty minutes. After that, no more would come. I practiced what I wrote, saying it out loud and asked Genny to evaluate me. Every time I did a trial run, Genny would say, "You just sound terrible; try to put some life into it."

The night of the retreat I still sounded no better according to Genny. The retreat started with a banquet that Friday night. I was the opening speaker for the retreat, which would continue until Saturday afternoon. I was seated at the head table and I could see that everyone was enjoying themselves; that's everyone accept me. Dozens of people filed by the head table to meet me and to tell me how eager they were to hear my testimony. God only knew what Ollie had told them about me. If only they knew what I knew. I knew that tomorrow will be a different story. After they heard me, they would probably all ignore me and wouldn't be so friendly any more. I felt too sick to eat; I could hardly stand to watch everyone else eat. The food looked really good, but who wants to eat when one is about to make oneself the fool of a lifetime?

Soon the meeting was on its way. I was glad, because I wanted to get it over with as quickly as possible. After the prayer and singing, Ollie went to the microphone to introduce me. He even shared some of my testimony, getting everyone pumped up. He called my name, and I stood to my feet trying to steady myself on my shaky legs. People stood up on their feet and applauded me. I introduced myself using all the dignity I could muster. I purposely spoke slowly to stretch out my speech. I fumbled my Bible open and waited for everyone to find the scripture. I then read my scripture and began to share what I had memorized. My own voice sounded pitiful to myself. All I could do was my best and trust the Holy Spirit to help me. Then something happened to me that I had never experienced before. Later I found out what it was; it is called the anointing. The Apostle John said,

> But the anointing which you have received from Him abides in you, and you have no need that anyone should teach you; as His anointing teaches you about every thing, and is true, and is no lie, just as it has taught you, abide in Him.
>
> 1 John 2:27

It just happened. Suddenly I started to feel confident and very happy. The words I spoke just flowed effortlessly out of my mouth with confidence and with authority. I no longer felt like that old nervous me. I had a burst of Holy Ghost energy. I felt in control like James Bond. God just gave me a secret weapon I did not know I had. My voice was no longer monotone. Every word that came out was carried forward on the wings of the Holy Ghost. People were sitting on the edge of their seats. I could see the smiles on their faces and heard the amens. I was sharing parts of my testimony that I did not even have in my notes. It was interesting even to me, since I have never heard it before. The time was simply standing still; I lasted beyond my own wildest expectation or Ollie's expectations. When I brought the meeting to a close, I asked Ollie to come and help me. Ollie glanced at me out the side of his eye as he took position next to me. "I thought you had nothing much to say," he mumbled. "Here you have been going for fifty minutes nonstop. You did a great job!" He almost shouted into the microphone. Everyone broke into applause with shouts of "Praise you, Jesus! Thank you, Jesus!"

When the applause started dying down Ollie and I started to pray for people; more of the leadership came forward to assist with praying for the needs. After everyone was done and things had wound down, Ollie called me to the side. He wanted to know what happened, because he said I did a great job. I explained to him that I really did not know what happened, "I just started to feel very confident and in control." I tried to explain, "It was like the words of what to say were just flooding into my mind just as fast as I could deliver them."

We were sitting down and he began to tell me that what I experienced was the anointing. "And you know what that means, don't you?" Ollie asked. I nodded my head that I did not know what that meant. "That means," Ollie said, "God is calling you to preach."

Well, I thought to myself, if preaching is going to be that easy, I suppose I could manage. My question would be, "Will God be there to anoint me every time if I had to preach?" I learned later that having the anointing also depended on me and how much I wanted to involve the Holy Spirit into my ministry.

Ollie had something he wanted to give me. He gave me a check for two hundred dollars. "That is yours from the F.G.B.M.F.I." he said. "This is normally what we give our speakers, but I also have some other money for you." He pulled a handful of notes from his pocket and said, "This here is from individuals who felt that God told them to give this to you." I looked at it, and my cup was running over. I had a lot more money now than what I had to come to the States with. And to think that back in South Africa, I was asking God to help me find a job while at Bible college. Ollie said, "There are several pastors and F.G.B.M.F.I. presidents who would like to speak to you tomorrow about coming to speak at their chapters."

A couple of hours ago I was nobody. I felt like that scared little barefoot boy from the farm who was the smallest in a one-teacher farm school. Every morning after traveling eight miles on my horse to school, I had to wait for one of the bigger boys to take me down from my horse. Now suddenly people of prominence want me to come to them to speak at churches and business men's chapters. Things were happening just a little too fast for me.

I was still nobody, with all my education and degrees. I knew deep down in my spirit that I was venturing into unknown territory. No one knew any better than I did how scared I was before the meeting had started. Inside me, my spirit was jumping with joy. Like David, God ordered His prophet to go and find a young boy taking care of his father's sheep and anoint him king of Israel. "God, I hope I can be a worthy servant. Thank you that you even used me tonight." If I live to be a hundred years old, I will always remember that night. That night God had set me free from fear; I pray that I shall never have to be afraid to do whatever God wants me to do ever again.

During the months that followed, Genny's and my speaking engagements picked up momentum and even though we had no transportation of our own, someone was always there to take us.

Evil Forces from the Dark Side Close In

And by the hands of the Apostles were many signs and wonders.

Acts 5:12

And I heard a loud voice saying in heaven Now has come the salvation and strength, and the kingdom of our God, and the power of his Christ: For the accuser of our bretheren is cast down, which accused them before God day and night. And they overcame him by the blood of the Lamb and their testimony, and they loved not their lives unto death.

Revelation 12:10–11

And He said unto them, I beheld Satan as lightning fall from heaven. Behold, I give unto you power to tread on serpents and scorpions, and over all the power of the enemy: and nothing shall by any means hurt you.

Luke 10:18–19

Hard as it was for me to realize, God had given me the same power and authority He gave the seventy disciples. Paul says, "There is one body, and one spirit, even as you are called into one hope of your calling; One Lord one faith, one baptism, one God and Father of all, who is above all, and through all in all" (Ephesians 4:4–6).

Daily God was teaching both of us, Genny and myself, enlarging our knowledge of Him and the finished work on Calvary. His spirit was truly teaching us and helping us daily to comprehend that Jesus had empowered us to go. It was a finished work. All I had to do was to accept the challenge as did His disciples. The Lord began to show me through His word that the church today does not have to be powerless. Why? Because He who is the Lord of the universe has not changed. How often have we as Christians heard people use the phrase Jesus the same yesterday, today and for ever? But really and truly even though they say they believe, they themselves don't believe that.

He is the same inside them. There are believers out there who do believe that Jesus is the same inside them as He was in His disciples, but they are few in number. I used to think that out there, somewhere was someone special that God was using. I was at one time constantly going to different meetings to find if that was the place where Jesus was manifesting His word, by following it with signs and wonders. But here, God was enlightening my mind and changing the way I always thought. I began to realize that I can never get good enough or smart enough or holy enough for God to even use me. He was never going to use me because I had become so special. Nothing I ever did could make me holy enough to stand in His presence.

In as much then as we have a great High Priest who has [already] ascended and passed through the heavens, Jesus

> the son of God, Let us hold fast to our confession [of faith in Him], For we do not have a High Priest who is unable to understand and sympathize and have a fellow feeling with our weakness and infirmities and liability to the assaults of temptation, but One Who has been tempted in every respect as we are, yet without sin. Let us then fearlessly and confidently and boldly draw near to the throne of grace, the throne of God's unmerited favor [to us sinners]; that we may receive mercy [for our failures] and find grace to help in good time for every need appropriate help and well timed help, coming just when we need it.
>
> Hebrews 4:14–16, AMP

Jesus is continuing until this day to do it for you and me. The reason why I can have unlimited access to the throne of God is because my High Priest is continually, day in and day out, there before the Father representing me. Covering me with His atonement. Hiding me behind His sacrifice. When God looks at me now through the veil of the blood of His only Son, all He can see is pure white, completely without sin. Worthy of God's love. Worthy of the Holy Spirit to dwell in me. Worthy to have my needs met. Worthy to be surrounded by ministering angels. Worthy to claim my healing. Worthy to walk in the Abrahamic covenant. God sees me worthy to be blessed. I am also God's son and I can sit at the same table with my heavenly family. All God's services are now at my disposal. All those ministering angels and the Holy Spirit who work for my Father and operate under His command, now also work for me and will operate under my command in Jesus' name.

Well then, I wondered, If the church, who represents all of God's children has so much power, why then are there so many powerless churches? Perhaps because we don't take God seriously? Because if I really believe Him, then I will never say anything contrary to His word. For instance, if God's word said that "By His stripes we were healed," will I confess God's word or my feelings? If God's word said that, "My God shall supply all my needs according to His riches in glory," will I believe my need, my creditor, or God's word?

I had a speaking engagement one particular night in 1973 at a Full Gospel Business Men's Fellowship International. But I had a very big problem. Several days before, Satan attacked me with something God had healed me of before. It was called Ulcerous Colitis. Doctors did not have a cure for it, but could treat it. When not treated, the ulcers would flare up and cause unbelievable pain and discomfort, including continuous cramping, diarrhea and bleeding in a matter of days. This particular day, I had been into the bleeding stage for a week. I certainly did not feel like going to the meeting. I felt weak and sick and could not eat. My stomach could not hold any food in. It was also a constant embarrassment to excuse myself to the rest room all the time. My body said, "Stay home. You are feeling too sick." Satan said, "Stay home. How can you honestly tell people tonight that you are healed when you are so sick? If you tell people you received healing, you will be telling a lie." Imagine the father of all lies reprimanding me about lying. But the Holy Spirit said: "Believe God's word; by His stripes you were healed. It is a finished work which Jesus had accomplished for you on Calvary. Go to the meeting and declare that Satan is a liar."

I thought by myself, "God, this is so hard to believe when one feels so sick." I felt that I just wanted to lie down and rather die." But I was also sick and tired of being sick, so I decided that if going to the meeting was going to help me to get victory over this thing I would go.

That night after Dale Barber picked me up for the meeting, I told Dale that I had been sick and was going to the meeting by faith. We had about one and a half hours to drive to the meeting place. The whole trip for me was nothing but agony and pain. Three times I had to use the rest room on the way. More than once I thought of asking Dale to speak in my place. But every time the Holy Spirit said, "If you want to gain the victory over Satan tonight, then you speak. Do it by faith." Jesus said,

> "For verily I say unto you, if ye have faith as a grain of mustard seed, ye shall say unto this mountain, remove hence to yonder place, and it shall be moved, and nothing shall be impossible unto you"
>
> Matthew 17:20

In faith that night I took the meeting. Even though I had not eaten in a week, I said to myself, "I don't feel healed, but I will confess I am healed to be in agreement with God's word, even though I felt like dying." When it came time for me to speak I had difficulty speaking loud enough to be heard. Twice they adjusted the volume to enhance the sound. My insides were hurting so bad I felt that I did not have enough breath in me to push the words out of my throat.

By faith I was standing there like an utter fool, when suddenly my words came bellowing out of me. Someone rushed to re-adjust the sound down and I was on my way. When I got home at 2:30 in the morning I realized that I had not been back to the rest room since the meeting had started at 6:30. That night the Holy Spirit taught me a very important lesson about faith. Faith is not just confessing God's word, and yes, whatever comes out of our mouths should always agree with the word of

God. But faith is also believing that Christ Jesus has already accomplished that which I have confessed, even before I could feel or visualize the outcome.

> So shall my word be that goeth forth out of my mouth: it shall not return unto me void, but it shall accomplish that which I please, and it shall prosper unto the thing whereto I send it.
>
> Isaiah 55:11

> Then said Jesus to those Jews which believed on Him. If ye continue in my word, then ye are my disciples indeed: And ye shall know the truth, and the truth shall make you free.
>
> John 8:31–32

Feelings do not count here; the only thing that can help me and set me free is the *word.* When I say what the Bible says, then I am in agreement with the *word,* and when I am in agreement with the *word,* then I am also in agreement with God's Son. When I am in agreement with God's Son, then He can plead my case for me before the Father, and accomplish that thing for which His *word* was sent. Because He said it, not I. All I have done was to believe Him and agree with His word.

> He personally carried the load of our sins in His own body when He died on the cross, so that we can be finished with sin, and live a good life from now on. For His wounds have healed ours.
>
> 1 Peter 2:24, TLB

On a Mission to Africa

> Whereby are given unto us exceeding great and precious promises: that by these ye might be partakers of the divine nature, having escaped the corruption that is in the world through lust.
>
> 2 Peter 1:4

Armed with ten thousand of Dr. Kenneth Hagin's books and tapes, and a stack of tapes donated to us by Kenneth Copeland, we started back to South Africa. By now I was no longer opposed to being a preacher. The word of the Lord was burning inside me like a fire and I had to tell it. I did not know where I could get started, but I had to trust the Lord. I was not going to return to my old job which I loved so much. Somehow everything that drove me to success in my profession was now driving me to preach. I knew in my spirit that God was going to use these books and tapes to reach people beyond my reach. That churches who would walk in the faith message, operating in signs and miracles would be birthed. I was not going to sell any of the materials I got, but distribute them free of charge. The first thing I did after I arrived back in South Africa was to telegram my resignation.

The first night back in Johannesburg I stayed with my

brother. Not knowing if he would listen to any of the tapes. I gave him some of Kenneth Copeland's tapes to listen to. My brother was raised in a Christian home, but was as far from God as one can get. He lived a life of lies and deceit, trying to become wealthy. About midnight his wife came into my room and said to me, "Your brother wants to talk to you."

I was unprepared for what I saw. His face was covered with tears. I asked him, "What is wrong?"

He replied, "I need to get saved, can you help me?"

His wife then said, "He has been listening to those tapes you gave him." I could feel the presence if the Holy Spirit in the room and told him to get out of bed and onto his knees. He prayed the sinner's prayer and accepted Christ.

In the end I gave all the tapes and books to a ministry in Johannesburg and personally know of many people who came to Rhema Bible College after that. Some of the people who came went back to South Africa and have started ministries, impacting the lives of thousands.

After much prayer and seeking the Lord on what to do, we felt led that we should move to Johannesburg and find a place to live. Genny and I prayed and asked God what we should do. He said, "Stay in Johannesburg, and sell your house in Cape Town."

We went to Cape Town and found our home that we had rented to the youth leader of the church, who stayed in it for a very small fee, all torn up. The drapes were torn, the brackets that held the drapes were torn out the walls, the walls had been written on. The wall paper was ripped. We left the house furnished, and we also found some of the furniture was damaged. My beautiful keyboard had been damaged by a blunt object. My neighbor told me that the couple was taking care of a family member, a large teenager with physiological and behavioral problems who would swing on the drapes and scratch up the walls. My first impulse was to see an attorney and drag them into court for damages. But I no sooner had the thought of doing that than the Holy Spirit entered the scene and reminded me of the words of Jesus.

> The law of Moses says, If a man gouges out another's eye, he must pay with his own eye. If a tooth gets knocked out, knocks out the tooth of the one who did it. But I say: Don't resist violence! If you are slapped on one cheek, turn the other too. If you are ordered to court, and your shirt is taken from you, give your coat too. If the military demands that you carry their gear for a mile, carry it two. Give to those who ask, and don't turn away from those who want to borrow.
>
> Matthew 5:38–42 RSV

Since I need the Holy Spirit always to guide me, it only makes good sense for me to follow Christ's directions. Instead of pursuing my tenants, Genny and I got some paint and painted the house. But I really did not want to stay in Cape Town any longer than I had to. We were both anxious to get settled and to get started in whatever ministry God was going to give us. So Genny and I decided to ask the Lord to send a buyer to purchase the house the day we got through painting.

After several days of painting, on Friday evening after we had been working the entire day we discovered that the government had passed a gas savings law in South Africa while we had been in America. The law required that all the gas stations closed Friday at 6 p.m. and did not reopen until Monday morning at 8 a.m. We were staying with Genny's folks about thirty minutes away. By the time we finished painting for the day it was 7 p.m. on a Friday. I pulled up at the gas station only to find that it would not be open again until Monday. There we were, sitting with an empty fuel tank. I did not know what I should do. Genny and I went to a hamburger place to get something to eat and to give us time to think over our dilemma. The idea struck us to pray and ask God to increase our gas so we could make it back to Genny's folks.

After we had our meal we got back into the car, but before we pulled out we prayed and asked the Lord that the fuel we had would be sufficient to get us home. I started the car and the needle showed that the tank was still as empty as it was when we stopped to eat, sitting on the "E." But about five miles out of the town, I noticed that the tank showed just a little more fuel. I pointed it out to Genny. After another five miles the tank was showing half. By the time we stopped at her folks' house the tank showed almost full. All excited we tried to share the miracle with Genny's folks. Her dad responded, "Your gauge just got stuck; God won't give you gas in your car."

Well, the miracle we felt was ours. It did not matter if no one believed us. We went back on Saturday to finish the painting on the house. Monday morning I called a few realtors to see if anyone had a buyer, but not one of them did. About 3 p.m. that Monday we completed the final painting touches on the house, and decided to pack up to go back to Johannesburg. I stopped for the first time on our way out of the town to fill up with gas. While pumping the gas, the owner of the station came up to me and said, "You have a phone call in my office." When I answered the phone it was one of the real estate offices. They said they had a cash buyer. If I took the buyer's offer they could process the paper work and give me my money that day. About three hours later when we left town we had the house sold and the money in our pocket.

Back in Johannesburg I tried to buy a house. One thing I forgot to do was to consult the Holy Spirit on the matter of buying a house. It is so easy to just fall right back in one's old ways of doing things and forget that the Holy Spirit has become one's life long partner. He is and stays with one all the time. I had seen a house in the paper and Genny and I went and looked at it. We instantly fell in love with it. The seller said he would finance the house himself, which meant we could move into it immediately. We made all the arrangements with the seller, who was going to get the paper work ready and call me to close on the deal.

A couple of days passed when I had a phone call. The seller of the house instructed me to bring my money and sign the papers for the house. While in the States I had bought myself a nice cross on a chain, which I was wearing around my neck that day. The seller knew that I had just returned from Bible college. But that day something very weird happened. When I stepped into the seller's office, he started to give me the papers to sign. Then all of a sudden his eyes were staring at the cross, locked onto it, almost magnetized. His hand stopped midway towards me with the papers for the house in his hand. Still staring at the cross, his face started to contort, wrenching out an almost satanic distortion, then the strangest thing happened. The man hissed like a snake and started to scream at me loudly saying, "Get out of my house, you Jesus devil, you! Out! Out! Out!" He continued screaming all the way to the front door of his house pushing me towards the door.

Driving back home I tried to analyze what had just happened. The Holy Spirit said to me, "The devil in him had recognized the Spirit of Jesus in you and trembled with fear at the sign of the cross. The man did not want to have to deal with you for a prolonged time. It is not that the devil doesn't want to deal with ministers or preachers. He can handle most of them. But when anyone has the Spirit of Jesus in them the devil trembles with fear."

I said, "Lord! Why did you not warn me not to do business with the man?"

"Simple!" the Lord said to me. "You did not ask me to guide you."

It is very easy at times to get sidetracked. I have to remind myself continuously that my life is in Him. After I gave my life to Jesus, I also surrendered my authority over my own affairs. I did this because I want Him to be in control of all my affairs. His input into my life will save me from undesirable circumstances that might come about because of my inability to recognize an errant decision that I might make. "For in Him we live, and move, and have our being; as a certain of your poets have said, For we are also His offspring" (Acts 17:28).

God wants continuous interaction with His children. Serving God requires that He has input in everything I do every day. God does not want to be left out of our daily lives, or daily decision making. Think about this. If one's life has become so entwined with the Lord's, do we insult Him when we leave Him out, or do we hurt His feelings, or just hurt ourselves? One might feel that God won't react but listen to what He says to Israel,

> Therefore shall ye lay up these my words in your heart and in your soul, and bind them for a sign upon your hand, that they may be as fronlets between your eyes. And ye shall teach them to your children, speaking of them when you sittest in your house, and when thou walkest by the way, and when thou liest down, and when thou risest up. and thou shalt write them upon the door posts of thine house, and upon thy gates.
>
> Deuteronomy 11:18–20

Continuous interaction from morning to night, while you walk, while you eat, even in bed. It is in the words of God that we have our life. It is in God's words that we have success and health and all our needs met. Jesus clarified the power and importance of God's Word further when he said, "It is the spirit that quickeneth; the flesh profiteth nothing: the words that I speak unto you, they are spirit, and they are life" (John 6:63).

Once I realized that I had left the Lord out of my buying a house, Genny and I got on our knees and asked the Lord to forgive us for not allowing Him to direct us, and to help us find a place. For some reason the Lord did not give us a house to purchase, but directed us into renting.

Our number one goal was to find a field of ministry. The Lord plainly told us to not build our own agenda, but to follow the leadership of the Holy Spirit. A door opened with a cousin of mine. She and her family were very eager to get closer to God. We started with meetings in their home, in a nearby city, Pretoria, which is the capital of South Africa. They both were prominent in the Dutch Reform church and had a lot of friends. The meetings started in their home and immediately drew a following from amongst their friends. After a while we had a few converts and also several who had received the baptism of the Holy Ghost. I wanted to reach out further to more people and the Lord directed me to set up a banquet at a hotel and get Ollie from the USA to come and help. I called Ollie and he said that the Lord had already confirmed to him through three different people that He should get ready to come to South Africa. "But I had a problem," Ollie said. "I don't have money to buy a ticket to fly."

Well, I could not help Ollie, because I could not afford to fly him out either. But in praying, the Lord said, "You offer to pay for Ollie and I will give you the money." I said, "Yes, Lord!" But I had no idea where the money would come from either. I called

Ollie to let him know that we would pay for him and that he should go ahead and book his flight and let me know the dates so I could start putting the banquet together. In the days that followed money slowly started to come in, one drop at a time. It came to two days before the due date for Ollie to fly out and we still needed four hundred Rand.

That morning I had a problem with my car and decided to stop by a garage that belonged to a believer. The brother who owned the garage started to work on my car to determine what the problem was and asked from under the car, "When is that American preacher suppose to come?"

I replied, "He is supposed to come in two days, but we have a slight problem."

"Oh! What is that?" he then wanted to know.

I said, "We are suppose to pay his airline tickets and we are still four hundred Rand short." For a moment there was dead silence.

The brother who was under the car sledded out and said, "You won't believe this, but just before you came in I was in my office and I asked God to show me where to give the four hundred Rand. You see, yesterday I sold a car and this morning the man brought me his money and four hundred Rand is the tithe. So it must be that God wants me to give it to you." I took the money he gave me and walked around the corner to a travel agent and transferred the money for Ollie's ticket to the airline in America.

I know somebody will say, "God won't do that for you, He has far more important things to do." Well, is that so? Then why was God so into Jonah's life that he had him in the belly of a fish? Why then did he help Abraham to pick his farm? Why did Jesus make wine at the wedding feast? Why did God send an angel to shut the mouths of the lions in the den Daniel was in? Is that any different?

It really is true that God loves us so much, that He sent His only begotten Son to pay the penalty for our sins. He also made us a part of His family; that's why we call ourselves God's children.

The tickets for the banquet had all sold. It was set up in one of Pretoria's fanciest hotels. Most of the people who were coming were members of the Dutch Reformed church. That night of the banquet God began to move in a powerful way. Ollie gave his testimony, which touched many people. When we started to pray for people's needs, people left, right and center were being filled with the Holy Ghost and speaking in tongues. It truly was a sight to behold. Business men and church deacons and their wives were lying on the floor in their fancy suits and dresses. The evening was dragging on over the estimated time and the banquet manager wanted to get the tables cleared. But because it was a religious service, out of respect, they were waiting for the meeting to end.

After 10:30 when they saw the meeting was still in full swing, he ordered the waiters and the waitresses to walk around the people on the floor and get the dirty dishes up. That was when the Holy Spirit began to zap them too. When these waitresses and bus boys went in to the meeting room and did not come out, the manager became furious and came storming in there to see what the holdup was. What he saw made him even more upset. Some of his staff was on the floor. Some were standing around speaking in tongues. He obviously had no idea what in the world had happened to his staff. He tried to tell one waiter to stop speaking in tongues and to get up the dishes, but all his shaking could not get the waiter's attention. He then came to me and said, "Do something, tell them to getup from the floor and get back to work."

I said, "I am not the one doing it to them and I can't tell them to stop. God has got a hold of them. If you hang around long enough, He will get a hold of you too." The manager left the room cussing and swearing and that was the last time that he would ever do a banquet for us.

Children of a Backslidden Catholic Priest

But when Jesus saw it, he was much displeased, and said unto them, Suffer the little children to come unto me, and forbid them not: for of such is the kingdom of God. Verily I say unto you, Whosoever shall not receive the kingdom of God as a little child, he shall not enter there in. And he took them up in his arms, put his hands upon them, and blessed them.

Mark 10:14–16

My neighbor was an Italian immigrant and business man. The day before Genny and I were leaving to attend a camp meeting in the Orange Free State, my neighbor came to me and asked me if we could watch their children, three boys. They had to go back to Italy to take care of some urgent business. So my neighbor came and asked me if we could help them out by taking care of their three boys. Genny and I discussed the situation and decided that we could help him out only if he would let the children go with us to the camp meeting. My neighbor readily agreed and assured me that he had no problem with that arrangement.

At the camp meeting they had facilities and staff to minister to the children. That arrangement worked very well, because it meant that parents did not have to be concerned about what children were doing. The camp meeting was going to last for ten days. But about halfway into the meetings one day, we were just coming out a service, when we heard a lot of noise. The sounds of screaming and laughter permeated the air. It did not sound like children playing; it was different. All the adults who were just coming out of their service had their ears kind of peaked to hear what the noise was all about. Some started to edge towards the sound, then some started running towards the sound. I myself started running.

When I reached the building where the sound came from, I tried to peek in through a window. What I saw could only be described as sounds from heaven. A sight so magnificently beautiful to observe, so precious. Children were dancing and jumping and singing and crying and praising God. It seemed that the angels from heaven were dancing with them. A radiant glow came from their little faces. All over the place there were little hands reaching straight up into the air, as if they were holding on to something invisible. The sight was so overwhelming. Moms and dads were so astounded, they were just standing there sobbing and crying and praising God all at the same time. That was for me without a doubt one of the most incredibly overwhelming and unforgettable experiences of my life.

Along with my children and all the other children were my neighbor's three children, who had also been baptized in the Holy Spirit. After the camp meeting, when we returned home, we returned the three boys to their parents. I did not try to explain to my neighbor what had happened to his children. But several days later he told me that the eldest, who was seven, had been getting onto him every time he uses fowl language. The boy also insisted that they pray and give thanks for their food before they eat. My Italian neighbor tried to shrug it off as if time would take care of it. But when the boy after a month still rebuked his father for cussing, they began to realize that what happened to their children was more than something that was just casually going to go away in time. It was real enough to the oldest little boy to keep reinforcing the two younger ones and keep reminding his dad. As the weeks passed and this little seven-year-old continued to embrace his commitment to Jesus, the whole family started to come to our home Bible studies because what they saw in their children was real. The father told me one day adults can still fake something, but not a child that small.

By the time we left South Africa for the second time, this family was just beginning to take small steps to come back to the Lord. The neighbor, who was at one time studying for the priesthood in the Catholic Church, said he saw the priests robbing old ladies from their money, taking all the inheritance a family would leave behind. Also at mealtimes at their parishes fellow priests would joke about how easy it was to get whatever they got. When he saw disturbing events like these happening, he began to realize that this kind of life was not for him.

Blackest Africa in God's Light

> The wolf also shall dwell with the lamb, and the leopard shall lie with the kid; and the calf and the young lion and the fatling together; and a little child shall lead them.
>
> Isaiah 11:6

One of the tribal ministers I was working with from time to time asked me to come and help him establish a church in a black township. The local school authorities had agreed that we could use the school to hold the meetings. People all over the neighborhood would send their children, to the meetings, but they themselves would not come. Every night at our meetings, the children would be there and sing and clap their hands. I tried to keep the preaching to a level where I felt sure that the children would understand it. Every night more children would give their lives to Jesus. However, none of the adults would come.

Often when we got to the school, the children would already be there waiting for us. Every night we, all the children, the minister, Genny and I would also pray and ask God to send the parents in. But the next day when we got there, only the children would be waiting for the service to start. The children would tell us that their parents were very happy about the meetings, because now they can drink and party each night at least until the service is finished. However, there was always one old lady who would be sitting all by herself in the back, the only other adult. As soon as the service was dismissed she would disappear.

This trend continued unchanged for several weeks until one day, shortly after the service started, the minister came to me and said, "That old lady who has been sitting in the back every night wants to give a testimony." When testimony time came, we gave the old lady the first opportunity to testify. She stood up and said, "From the first night I came here I have been asking God to heal me, and you have also been praying for me. I have been a patient in this hospital as a long-term patient for seven years. I had tuberculosis and they told me that I would have to spend the rest of my life in this hospital. When I heard about the services, I asked them if I could go. They said I could as long as I don't make close contact with any people. After the first couple of nights I felt that God had healed me and I asked them to please take some x-rays and see if I was healed. Today the results of those x-rays showed that I don't have any trace of tuberculosis left in my body. The doctors discharged me today after seven years."

A miracle was all it took to break the satanic stronghold the enemy had on that neighborhood. Every one in the township knew who this old lady was. After her discharge from the hospital, people would see her walking on the street, and she would tell them how that God had healed her. After that, more and more people started to show up nightly for the meetings. Last I heard, that pastor had built a church and had a strong congregation in that township.

What I share in my book may not be acknowledged as ordinary events. But the reason I share my life is to show that God can move through anyone who is committed and willing to follow Him. One does not have to be a Billy Graham or an Oral Roberts to accomplish works in the kingdom of God. I feel that too often God's people think that they don't have enough prestige with God to be worthy of doing things that will yield eternal rewards. Please don't think that. God certainly is not into big things. God is in all things, but especially into small things. Jesus ministered to the woman at the well first, before He ministered to the town. We can minister to our neighbor first, or a friend at work. God is also into "one on one" ministry.

In Acts chapter eight we read the story of how God had Philip to minister to only one person. An Ethiopian who was traveling on a cart. The importance God places on "one on one" ministry was evident by the fact that the Holy Spirit lifted Philip and transported him back home after his mission was completed. There were no miracles that took place. There were no healings that took place. Only great revelation knowledge, which after all is the most important event in any Christian's life. The knowledge that God sent His only begotten Son to save you and me. The Ethiopian was baptized in to the body of Christ by Philip and that was the whole sum of that story. Now why would God intervene in the middle of an ongoing revival to send Philip on a one man crusade to save only one soul? I can tell you why I think, Why? One soul at a time to God is very important that is why.

Hidden Treasures of the Secret Kingdom

> Lay not up for yourself treasures upon the earth, where moth and rust doth corrupt and thieves break through and steal. But lay up for yourself treasure in heaven, where neither moth or rust doth corrupt, and where thieves do not break through nor steal.
>
> Matthew 6:19–20.

A year had gone by since we had come back to South Africa and the Lord had slowly begun to tell both Genny and me to return to the USA. Genny and I did not want to be hasty or move out of God's perfect will for us, so we set aside time for fasting and praying. We had both felt that the Lord wanted us to go back to America, but just to be absolutely sure that we heard right, we fleeced the Lord.

The Lord had told us not to store any of our belongings and not to ship any of our belongings. Instead God said to sell what we can and give the rest away. The fleece we put before the Lord was, "God, if this is what you want us to do, please send people to buy our stuff, without me having to place an advertisement in the newspaper." We did not give God a time limit, just that. I really did not expect anything to happen. After I had time to think about my prayer, I even thought that my prayer was unfair to God. It is hardly fair to want to sell one's things without advertising.

The next day Genny went to her hairdresser to get her hair done. She had been going to the same hairdresser for a year and developed a ministry there. It had all started when they found out that Genny had been to Bible college in America. The people in the hairdressing salon just started to ask some questions. Often the kind of questions they didn't feel comfortable asking their minister. You know with most people, immaterial of how upbeat they come across, if you talk to them long enough they begin to loosen up. Then you find that they, meaning just about everyone, have a cross that they carry. Most people don't really want to talk about it, because they have already accepted it as their cross for life. Of course, as children of God we have all learned that the only One who can lighten one's cross is Jesus. Well, after Genny had been going there for a while people started to open up to Genny and Genny began to point them to Jesus. A women's Bible study was born out of that. Some of the ladies would bring their Bibles to the salon and have Bible study while getting their hair done.

On several occasions an emergency of a spiritual nature would occur when someone needed urgent counseling. Usually they would call Genny. One day when such an emergency occurred, Genny was asked to get there as fast as she could. One of the ladies was in tears over something that had happened. Genny was given a room in the back to counsel the lady in. The Lord began to move on her during the time she and Genny were praying together, which stirred up quite a commotion. Everyone in the shop, including the clients, moved up closer to the door to hear what the commotion was all about. In sobs and tears, the lady with Genny was asking Jesus to come into her heart. After

Genny had taken care of what she was there for, she opened the door and there were some of the staff and clients with their ears pressed to the door and eyes filled with tears. Surprised, Genny explained what had happened and asked if there was anyone else who wanted to ask Jesus into their hearts. Surprisingly, there were several.

When Genny went there to get her hair done on this particular day, she said to the ladies that we were thinking of going back to America. The conversation led to someone asking, "What will you do with your furniture?"

"Sell it all," Genny replied. Several of the ladies who overheard the conversation then wanted to know if they could come and look at the furniture.

Genny, who was totally unprepared for what would happen next, said, "Yes, you can."

In minutes they were ready to close the shop and come over to the house. Taken totally by surprise, Genny said, "Do all of you want to come right now?"

"Yes we do, we don't want to wait, otherwise we might miss out on a good deal," they said.

Stunned, Genny said, "Give me an hour to go home and get ready?" They agreed and Genny rushed home. As soon as she opened the door she said to me, "Hurry, let's get some prices on the furniture, there are a few ladies from the hairdresser who will be here in an hour to look at what we've got for sale."

I looked at Genny and said, "We can't sell the stuff today. We only put the fleece out to God this morning. Besides, we first need to book our passage and get packed and-"

Genny put her hand up and said, "That is okay. They are only coming to look. Just put some prices on the stuff we know we will have to sell. We will also tell them that if they want anything, they can only get it when we move out of the house."

That sounded reasonable to me and we started to put prices on everything. I decided not to sell anything cheap and to put the prices high. I thought that way not too many people would be interested. In my own mind, I was not convinced that going to America was the right thing to do. Somehow I was still hoping that God would intervene and say, "Stop, you don't have to go." In my own mind I thought that there was more for me to do in Africa than in America.

Genny and I hurriedly put some prices on. One hour later several cars pulled up in the front yard. For the next hour my house became totally chaotic. It was as if we had offered each of them a share of the sweepstakes. Everyone was trying to be first to say what they wanted. I put my hand up and said, "Ladies, please, why don't you just look, there is no rush, go home and think about what you want and let me know tomorrow."

"We can't do that," a few shouted, "we have to decide now."

I said, "Ladies! Even if you decide tonight, you won't be able to get anything; we still have to use the stuff until we move out." I explained that I had not booked our air passage and neither had I given notice to move out of the house. But my objections were to no avail. Within one hour from the time they came in the door all the furniture was spoken for and I was holding several thousand dollars in my hand.

After they had all gone I said to Genny, "Can you believe that they all paid and agreed to leave the stuff until we move out?" Johannesburg is a big city like New York. It is quite possible that one could run an advertisement for weeks and never even get one call. When you open the classified pages there, it is literally like opening the telephone book. "One hour," I said. "This time God must really mean business."

Genny did not object that God had told her to sell all the big stuff. But when she began to look at all her wedding presents and gifts that were given to her over the years, she discovered that there were a few things that she could not part with or bring along as luggage. After thinking about it she decided that God did not really mean it when He said to sell everything and not to keep or ship anything and give away what did not sell. "The only things you keep," God said, "are the things you take within your luggage." The next day we had more people come to the house. We even sold some of the children's toys and clothing that could not fit into our luggage. But the list of valuables that Genny could not part with also grew bigger and bigger.

Genny kept adding something here and something there. The day before we had to move out of the house, she had a friend to come by the house and pick up all the things she decided the Lord wouldn't mind if she kept. The few things filled the man's van chock and block. He was going to store her things in his garage. The next morning around eight a phone call. The man on the phone was the friend who was storing Genny's things. "I have some bad news," he started out. "Something occurred that had never happened to us before." He went on to say, "Last night we had a break-in. When I got up this morning, I found that all the stuff I had to store for you had been stolen." After a minute of silence, Genny asked him, "Did they take a lot of your things?" "No," he said. "They did not take anything of mine, only yours."

After the conversation was over, Genny simply said, "I guess the Lord really did not want me to keep anything."

> Are not two sparrows sold for a farthing? And not one of them shall fall to the ground without your Father; but the very hairs on your heads are numbered. Fear ye not therefore, ye are of more value than many sparrows.
>
> Matthew 10:29–31

Face to Face with Death

Wherein ye greatly rejoice, though now for a season, if need be ye are in heaviness through manifold temptations

1 Peter 1:6

Through faith we understand that the worlds were framed by the word of God, so that things which are seen were not made of things which do appear

Hebrews 11:3

It was the end of May 1975. I was in Tulsa by myself for the graduation ceremony. Genny and the children stayed behind in South Africa, where Genny was going to auction the American car we had imported from the United States to South Africa. The actual date of the auction was still a month away; coming to the States ahead of them would give me the time to find us a place to live in America. A Christian brother who lived in Tulsa had a furnished house which was on the market for sale and he said we could move in the house and stay until the house sold. Taking the brother up on his offer would allow me more time to find and select a suitable house for my family. I contacted Genny immediately to tell her I found a temporary house. It would only be good for a few months, but would do for then.

However, the day I called her she gave me some terrible news. Michael, one of my twin boys, was in the children's hospital in Johannesburg. Genny explained how Michael, then nine years old, woke up one morning unable to get out of bed. He was paralyzed on the left side of his body. His left leg and arm and also the facial muscles on the left side of his face, even his left eye, were drooping and he was unable to move his eye lid. The left side of his mouth stayed open and he was unable to close it. My first thought was God had given us one sign after another to go to the United States. I was certain I was in God's will. So this attack without a shadow of a doubt was the work of Satan to bring doubt into our hearts. The only option I had was to continue to walk by faith. After wrestling with my own thoughts for a while God gave me strength in this scripture: "Through faith we understand that the worlds were framed by the word of God, so that things which are seen, were not made of things which do appear" (Hebrews 11:3).

To me God was saying, "Don't fear. It is not as bad as it sounds. Have faith. I am with you." The first thing I usually do when Satan gets into the picture is counterattack, and what better way than to call on the body of Christ, so I did just that. I called a few churches and asked for prayer; that night I also went to a Bible study and asked the believers to intercede for Michael. We claimed God's word which says: "And the prayer of faith shall save the sick, and the Lord shall raise him up, and if he have committed sins, they shall be forgiven him" (James 5:15).

God gave me peace in my heart with the assurance that everything was going to be all right. Another week passed before I spoke to Genny on the phone again, at which time she told me that Michael was out of the hospital. She continued to tell me how the doctors were unable to diagnose Michael's condition and suggested she take him home. The doctors said it was not possible to treat something if you did not know what you were treating. She also told me that after she returned with Michael to my dad's home, where she was staying. My dad, who has gone to be with the Lord since, told her to sit Michael on a chair, which she did. He then laid his hands on Michael and commanded the demon to come out. Simultaneously my mother's maid, who was a from the Zulu tribe, for whom it was customary to communicate with spirits, let out a scream at the top of her voice, saying, "Daar gaan die duiwel by die deur uit," which in English means there the devil is going out of the door.

After the demon came out of Michael, he sat up and said he was hungry. His facial muscles immediately returned to normal. He got off of the chair and started walking towards the kitchen to get food to eat. This is the same child who for two weeks now had been unable to hold down any food or fluids. Who had to be carried from the hospital to the car, unable to walk, now miraculously walks!

That day I began to realize that the power to cast out devils did not belong to a small select group of believers. No, the power to cast out devils belonged to every child of God. God also honors and empowers every one of His children who accepts the commission Jesus gave to His followers. Jesus said to His disciples, "Heal the sick, cleans the lepers, raise the dead, cast out devils, freely ye have received, freely give" (Matthew 10:8).

I was beginning to think about it and wondered if we as believers could truly grasp how Jesus disabled Satan, and how He empowered the church to use His authority to bind and restrict the activities of the demon world. If we understand how to use the power that God has given his children, we may be better in helping those who are sick and afflicted.

It was a month now that I was in Tulsa separated from my family. It was midnight. I had just crawled into bed and under a thin cover, when a phone call from South Africa came in. It was my cousin's husband on the other end. He called to say that the phone lines across the ocean had been out of order for several days, and that he was just then able to get through to me for the first time. He told me Genny and the children had left South Africa twelve hours ago for the United States, but because a hurricane at sea had cut the telephone lines they were unable to get in touch with me. He also said that Genny had made arrangements to stay at the Holiday Inn nearest the airport in New York, where she would remain until she could get in touch with me. I thanked him for taking the trouble to let me know, and within about five minutes I was in my car and on the road from Tulsa to New York. Those days in 1975, the speed limit on the highways was still around seventy-five miles per hour, and although the car I was driving was an older model Olds 98, I traveled all the way at the maximum speed allowed. I prayed as I drove, asking the Lord to keep me safe. The trip seemed to take forever, but about twenty hours later I found myself on New York's freeways.

Talk about happy, we were all very happy once we were reunited and all together as a family. Genny told me that they had a safe trip, but the boys were a handful, always wanting to get into stuff. Their running and playing just gave their mother a fit. However, God was good. He helped her with the selling of the car, which we had bought for three thousand dollars in the States, and sold for ten thousand five hundred dollars in the auction in South Africa.

Once we arrived in Tulsa, no one was particularly impressed with the house I secured as a temporary residence, but we hoped it would do until we could find something else. A few days after Genny and the children had settled in, Genny received an invitation to be a speaker at a women's convention in Colorado. She was to leave in a few days, but the night before Genny had to leave, I was the speaker for the F.G.B.M.F.I. chapter. That was the night that Dale Barber drove me to the meeting and I felt so weak, and had to go to the rest room every thirty minutes or so. Well, that night you will remember God gave me complete victory over the enemy, and I had not been sick with that symptom since. So here I was about fifteen months later going back to the same F.G.B.M.F.I. chapter. I had totally forgotten about that night when God healed me. That was until I was reminded.

After my arrival at the meeting I saw several people who still remembered me. Every one I spoke to seemed really glad to see me and we had a great meeting. After a successful meeting, I stared to make my way back home. It was about one in the morning. I could already see the sky lit up from Tulsa's city lights. Fifteen more minutes or so and I would be home, when all of a sudden I realized that I had someone other than the Holy Ghost in the car with me. The realization completely took me by surprise.

You know the one thing in this life we are going to have to deal with on a regular basis is Satan himself, who Jesus said is the accuser of the bretheren, who accuses them before God day and night. That night however, I was going to find out for myself, just how much of a pain in the butt Satan could be. God's word tells us:

> "Be sober, be vigilant, because your adversary the devil, as a roaring lion, walketh about seeking whom he may devour. Whom resist stedfast in the faith, knowing that the same afflictions are accomplished in your brethren that are in the world"

1 Peter 5:8, 9

One thing I have come to realize is, never make the mistake to think the battle between you and the enemy is ever over; he will come again and again, no matter how many swipes you take at him. He is like an irritating fly. Someone said one time that for some reason no one ever told the devil that Jesus won the battle over him at Calvary and somehow he is still under the misconception that he has a chance. The biggest mistake we as Christians can ever make is to forget that Jesus won the Battle for us at Calvary. We must remind ourselves every day that the power of God's word belongs to us. We also have to remind the devil that we know that he, is powerless. My advice to myself when he attacks is to confess by saying, "Devil from this day on, I will not fear you, and I command you in the name of Jesus to stay off God's property. I am God's property. Every time I become aware of your presence, I will command you to bow your knees to Jesus, and we both know how much you would hate to do that. I command you now, before you leave out the door, bow your knee to Jesus and get out of my life. I will do this every day until I am satisfied that Satan is gone. Then I confess and say, "I thank you, Father in heaven, that you have not given me a spirit of fear but of power and of love and a sound mind. I will fill my thoughts with joy and happiness and I will overcome each day because God's word says that 'Greater is He that is in me than he that is in the world.'"

However, that night in my car on my way home was not a happy night. I was getting closer to home and I could already see the lights of Tulsa in the far distance when without any warning, I felt warm liquid dripping out of me and on to the seat where I was sitting. It did not take long for me to realize that I was sitting in a pool of blood. I felt no pain and no discomfort in any way. Suddenly the realization struck me. It was him, the same devil, because tonight, I was ministering at the same

F.G.B.M.F.I. chapter where I was at the night God delivered me from the bleeding. I thought, "Lord Jesus! is it possible that the same demon has been sitting there in the same place where I left him fifteen months ago, Is that possible? Could it be that when he saw me tonight that he decided to get back into my body; is it possible?" For many years in my ignorance I thought that evil spirits only lodge with people who don't pray or serve God, or who had fallen into sin. But I had done nothing like that. I have been serving God with all my heart. The one scripture that came to my mind was in Matthew 12:43–45:

> When the unclean spirit is gone out of a man, he walketh through dry places, seeking rest, and findeth none. Then he said I will return into my house from whence I came out; and when he is come he findeth it empty, swept, and garnished. then goeth he, and taketh with himself seven other spirits more wicked than himself, and they enter and dwell there: and the last state of that man is worse than the first.

Was that the case with me, I wondered, but I also thought that maybe Jesus was talking about someone backsliding. For the life of me I could not think of anything I did to give Satan any opportunity. Then I recognized what Jesus was saying. Jesus gave no indication that the person had committed any sin. In fact the person in the scripture had just gotten off his knees. He had been talking to God. His sins were all forgiven. He was clean, swept, pure, garnished with God's love and His word. I was still pondering the thought when the story of Job flashed in my mind. Job, the Bible say was a *righteous* man. Suddenly I knew what to do, I had to call for help, I had to talk to my *High Priest!* Because if this is a test I am going to need some serious help or else I could get into serious trouble. Hebrews 4:15–16 has this to say about calling on our high priest for help.

> For we have not a High Priest which cannot be touched with the feeling of our infirmities; but was in all points tested like as we are, yet without sin. Let us therefore come boldly unto the throne of grace, that we may obtain mercy, and find grace to help in time of need.
>
> Hebrews 4:15–16

My invitation by the *Word of God,* when I am in desperate need is to come boldly. Because up there in the courts of heaven, I have someone who will petition God on my behalf. Petition God to set me free from this evil spirit. The name of my high priest is *Jesus.* One thing I have learned over the years is that Satan never waits for an invitation, he just comes in and makes himself at home in you. One other thing I remembered: Satan always will try to use the same ploy, to sow doubt in your mind. As soon as I got home I ran to the rest room, my backside was dripping with blood, I cleaned myself and stuffed a lot of toilet tissue in my underwear to catch the bleeding. Even when I bled before, it had never been that bad. By the time I got myself settled, it was after two in the morning. Four more hours and it will be six o'clock, at which time Genny will be leaving for Colorado, where she was scheduled to minister at this women's conference in Vail, Colorado. I found a chair to sit in; I still felt somewhat confused by what was happening to me. I think it is a human thing to start to feel sorry for oneself. Instead of coming boldly before my high priest, I felt sad and humiliated, depressed and rejected, and wondered why God did not command his Angels to protect me? I was exercising that old feel sorry for oneself syndrome, saying, "Why me Lord?" For that moment I forgot what God's word had promised me. God's word never promised me that it would be easy, but rather it promises a crown of glory for the overcomer. "Blessed is the man that endureth temptation: for when he is tried, he shall receive the crown of life, which the Lord hath promised to them that love him" (James 1:12).

The next morning early before Genny left, she reminded me that I had the power given to me by Christ to overcome this attack and before she left we agreed in prayer for my healing.

The days were passing slowly. I purposely left my schedule open, to take care of the children that week. After Genny left, I also called churches for prayer support. But instead of getting better, I became worse with the passing of each day. I had continuous stomach cramps. By the time Genny returned home one week later I was so sick I had people sitting with me all day. I had such severe pain that I was grunting at times. Every bowel movement felt like a trip to Hell, and back. Sweat was forming on my face as razor sharp pains in my bowel caused me to double over with pain during these frequent bowel movements. What was worse was the fact that I had to have a bowel movement about every twenty minutes to release blood; which felt like daggers piercing me up and down my colon. By now I was also too weak to walk by myself. I had to depend on somebody taking me to the bathroom every twenty minutes. It was impossible for me to eat any food, in fact I held nothing down. Even the sips of water I took so my throat would not feel so dry, would cause me to vomit. Well, I don't profess knowing too much about evil spirits, but I was determined that one way or the other Satan was going to find himself in a dry place. My mind was made up. I was going to wait until God rescued me; either Satan is going to kill me or I am going to get rid of him. For now I am still holding onto my faith, and I am holding onto the scripture in 1

Peter 2:24: "Who his own self bare our sins in his body on the tree, that we, being dead to sins, should live unto righteousness, by whose stripes ye are healed."

It is there in the word just as plain as can be, that Jesus took care of my sickness on the cross at Calvary. Well, if Jesus took care of it, then why am I in so much pain? Why? Why? Why? I already knew that Jesus gave me the power and the responsibility to exercise His word and cast this devil out, but he was not moving. I kept confessing, over and over, hundreds of times each day, "I am healed, by his stripes I am healed." I also tried to search for an answer; I had to know the truth, I had to know why I was sick. I read and read and read God's word, and came upon this scripture. Ephesians 6:12–13:

> For we wrestle not against flesh and blood, but against principalities, against powers, against rulers of the darkness of this world, against spiritual wickedness in high places. Wherefore take unto you the whole armor of God, that ye may be able to withstand in that evil day and having done all to stand.

Just because I prayed, and prayed and prayed, did not necessarily mean that the fight was won and the battle was over. The word very specifically is saying to us, when you have done all you can do, stand, stand on that confession. I kept on saying to myself I am healed! 'God's word says it, I believe it, Jesus paid for it and I stand on it.' The enemy came back over and over to say to me, "Did God say he would heal you? Do you feel healed? Why would God even bother to listen to you; you are the least of his concerns." On and on the Devil talked to me saying, "God has a universe to run, and you are here bothering Him with something so insignificant, He's not even hearing you." Every day Satan came back to plant seeds of doubt. Over and over he would asked, "Are you feeling better yet?" All I would say, "By His stripes I am healed, because I don't trust my feelings, no, I only trust the word of God. I will continue to stand! Stand! Stand!"

All I could do was to stand, stand on the promises, stand on my faith; I did not feel healed but I stood on that everlasting promise of that never failing Word, of the eternal God, whose word remains the same, yesterday, today and for ever.

Jesus very specifically told us how important it was to be careful what we say,

> I tell you, on the day of judgment men will render account for every careless word they utter; for by your words you will be justified, and by your words you will be condemned.
>
> Matthew 12:36–37 RSV

I had to agree with what God said in His word. His word said that I was healed. However, my body said that I was sick. I had a choice here; should I believe what I was feeling or should I believe God's word?

Please, anyone who reads this book, I am not trying to tell you what to do. This book is simply an account of my personal involvement and the stand I took on my own behalf. You have to follow your own convictions.

For ten days I had confessed God's word with undying belief that He would pull me through. But on the other hand I was also convinced that if I did not come through, I would rather die and go to be with the Lord, than to admit defeat to Satan.

It was around midnight of the tenth day; I had no strength at all and I was too weak to talk. When Genny and the children talked to me I could only reply in a whisper. In ten days of bleeding, I had dehydrated to the point that my skin would stick together. The pain was so overbearing, I finally gave up hope of making it through alive. I had no fight left; I thought; "that's it! I am going to die and I may as well get some painkillers to ease the pain." I asked Genny to please call my good friend Dr. Duffy to come and give me something for the pain. I just had no strength left to continue the fight. While Genny called the doctor I whispered a prayer. 'Dear Lord.' I said, "please forgive me but I am almost dead, and can't fight any more." It took Dr. Duffy only a few minutes to get to my house. He walked in and immediately took my blood pressure and said what I already felt. He called Genny to the side and told her that I would be dead before morning unless he could take me to the hospital and give me an immediate blood transfusion. He also told Genny that I had lost too much blood for him to register a blood pressure. Genny, knowing how hardheaded I was and having refused all help this far, said that she would try to convince me, but she doubted that I would go. What she did not know was that I had already given up the fight. She walked into the bedroom and said, "You can go with Dr. Duffy and get a blood transfusion, or I can call your children and you say goodbye to them, because you will not live to see the sun come up in the morning, and as far as getting something for the pain, Dr. Duffy said that even one Aspirin will kill you, so what will it be?" She really did not need to have taken that tone with me, because I was beyond fighting. I said, "let him take me to the hospital." Minutes later they had carried me and placed me on the back seat of Dr. Duffy's car and I was on my way to the hospital. Once at the hospital I was carried into emergency and placed on a stretcher. I was wheeled behind a curtain and the nurses drew a sample of blood from a prig on my finger. I felt light headed, my head was swimming. I only caught glimpses of activity around me. I felt like I was floating in and out of consciousness.

Suddenly there was no one, I was by myself. I was lying on a bed with a white curtain drawn around the bed and I started to feel strangely wonderful. All the pain was gone. For a second I wondered if I had died. Why was I feeling so good, no pain at all? I felt happy, I wanted to get out of the bed and walk around. Then the thought struck me that, "Perhaps I was already dead." I felt myself with my hands; I wanted to feel if I was still in my body. I thought I was feeling too good to be alive; no pain. What is happening to me? I must have been lying there for thirty minutes. Suddenly the curtain pulled open. The nurse came in and wanted to take my blood pressure for the second time. "I have to do it for the record." she said, "The Dr. has ordered some blood for you, we are now waiting for it to get here." She pumped the little gadget, looked at it, listened to my heart, then for some unknown reason without saying a word she dropped everything and ran out of the room without any explanation.

Puzzled, I thought well maybe I did die, and she just realized that she was talking to a corpse. Seconds later Dr. Duffy came storming into my cubicle and started to pump the little gadget himself, then looked at the gauge. He let the air out and started the same procedure again, then shouted at the nurse, "Go call the blood bank! If they have not sent the blood yet, cancel it!" Dr. Duffy looked at me and asked, "Can you tell me what has happened to you?" I did not know either.

I answered, "I feel good, I have no pain."

He interrupted as if he did not hear me and said, "Thirty minutes ago you registered no blood pressure, and now your blood pressure is normal, in fact it is more than normal, your blood pressure registered like that of a new born baby."

"All I know," I said, "is that I have never felt this wonderful before; it just happened, I can't tell you how."

Then he said, "God has given you a miracle, you are healed." He started to examined me more thoroughly, pressed on my stomach. "Do you feel any pain?" he asked.

I said, "No."

After he got done poking me he said, "I am going to keep you here for a few days, I know that God has just healed you, but you are still weak, so let us keep you here for a few days and tomorrow the intern specialist can take a look at you also." Dr. Duffy then told me that he had called an intern specialist to talk to me in the morning. He said he tried to get him to see me that evening, but when Dr. Duffy told the intern specialist that I had been at home for the past ten days refusing medical help, to which he replied, "If anyone is that stupid they deserve to die, I will see him tomorrow if he is still alive."

The next day was a Friday, and around nine that morning the intern specialist was sitting by the side of my bed talking to me. He said that as far as he could tell all the bleeding had stopped, but they will keep me for a few days to monitor the situation. The intern specialist wanted to know why did I not get help sooner? Well, I did not really want to discuss that with him; it was a matter between me, God and the devil. In my opinion it was not just a sickness, but a spirit that caused me all the pain and bleeding. I could not talk to the intern specialist about it, because I did not think he would have understood. I replied simply by saying, "I don't want to talk about it." The next question he had, he wanted to know if I had insurance, and how would I pay for the treatment. I wanted to say, "What treatment?" But I didn't, instead I said, "I travel and I preach, and I am sure my Boss will give me the money to pay as soon as I get the bill." That apparently was not good enough for him, he wanted to know who my boss was. I told him I had just one boss, whose name is God.

I think just about then he started to get aggravated, and said, "Here, I will leave these forms with you, please fill them out, and the hospital needs the name and address of where to send the bill to."

To which I replied, "Dr., if you don't mind, please don't leave the forms with me, I don't really even know what my own address is, why don't you just send the bill to Dr. Duffy, and I will get the bill from him." It's not easy to stand on God's Word, and then have to explain to unbelievers, why one does strange things.

It felt good to feel better again, and even though hospital food leaves a lot to be desired, I still enjoyed it, especially after ten days of not eating. I ate everything they brought me and asked for more.

The next day we faced another dilemma. Genny came to see me; she sat on the side of the bed and said, "I have all four the children and all our belongings in the back of the car, the landlord came to the house last night and told me to be out of the house by noon today. He said he had someone who wanted to buy the house, and we needed to be out by noon." I looked at her with unbelief and said, "Did you tell him your husband is in the hospital and you have nowhere to go?" She said, "Yes, I told him, all he said, it was not his problem, he said either I am out or he will be there to help me out." Can you believe that? And the man calls himself a believer. Well, what can I say. The enemy is at it again. One knows the Lord will take care of His own, but can't Satan at least give one some breathing space? Through God's word I have come to the understanding, not to necessarily blame people for things the enemy is trying to do through them. You have weak believers and then you have strong believers. If things are not working out in the way one anticipated, there is, and will always only be one person you need to talk to, his name is Jesus. If people do you wrong, don't get mad at them; get mad at the devil; and the ones who have done wrong, pray for them. This is what Jesus said:

> Ye have heard that it hath been said, an eye for an eye, and a tooth for a tooth. But I say unto you that ye resist not evil: but whosoever shall smite thee on the right cheek, turn to him the other also. And if any man will sue thee at the law, and take away thy coat, let him have thy cloak also. And whosoever shall compel thee to go one mile, go with him twain.
>
> Matthew 5:38–41

Is that what is expected of me? Does the Lord really want believers to be humiliated, or always to be the least? Well, you know we live in a society where many people are without love or concern for others. Jesus is saying to us not to be like them. I have to love them with the love of the Lord even when they don't love me back.

Instead of fuming and foaming at the mouth about how unfair the brother was, I took Genny's hand and we talked to Jesus about our problem. After we prayed Genny went downstairs to the hospital lobby and got us a newspaper. We did not see much for rent, but there was one advertisement for a trailer that was fully furnished. I said to Genny, "Call them and see if it is still available." She picked up the phone by the side of my bed and called. The man said the trailer was still available, and that he required excellent references.

"References?" That we did not have, but our God is a great God and he takes care of his own. When Genny got to the trailer park, the man was waiting for her, she told him that she has only been here less than a month, and she does not have any references. The man looked at her and said lady, "I can detect the accent, you are from South Australia." Genny said, "You are right, that's where I went to school in Adelaide." The man gave her the keys and she was able to move her things in immediately, no references required.

Monday morning the hospital said I could go home and Genny came and got me. I was glad to be back *home,* ha! ha!. We prayed together and thanked the Lord for his provision, even though the house was roach infested and had a smell to it, even the furniture looked pathetic like its best days were long gone. Yes, we were thankful for God's provision, but we also asked the Lord to show us if he had a place more suitable. There are two things I strongly believe in as a child of God.

> Be satisfied with what you have; there is no need to go around complaining all the time, Paul says this, "Not to speak in respect of want: for I have learned, in whatsoever state I am, therewith to be content."
>
> Philippians 4:11

Now I realize that the comforts of home are not always available in the same way one is used to. When one is traveling and holding seminars, or ministers in tribal communities in Africa, or just staying for a few days with strangers, there will always be some things that may not appeal to one's usual taste or offer the same comforts one is used to having at home. But why complain? If that is what God arranged for you to have, be satisfied.

Genny tells me that I like to live on the edge. Back in Africa a friend and I went on a hunting safari with some Bushmen. The

Bushmen hunt with a bow and arrow. Their method is to run alongside their prey and shoot the arrow into the heart of the animal they hunt. My friend and I did not think we could keep up with the Bushmen, so we followed them in a pickup truck. After the prey falls, the Bushmen quickly remove the poisonous arrow from the animal, to prevent the poison from spreading. After the meat is cut up into smaller chunks, the family gets together to start cooking and eating. First they send one of their youngsters to get fire buried in the ground, as to light a fire to cook on. After the meat is cooked {half burned and half raw} the eating begins. Depending on the size of the catch, the eating can continue throughout the night and into the next day. The Bushman simply eats until he drops down in a state of unconsciousness. They may lay like that for hours. As soon as one wakes up he start to eat again. This will continue until they have eaten all the food they have. The Bushmen has such a big stomach that when he is full it is hard for him to stay balanced on his feet. But when he is hungry his stomach simply hang: over his knees, just a huge empty skin. Since they don't have anywhere to store their food, they use their stomachs for storage.

Over the years I discovered how different the world cultures are. Different cultures operates on a completely different value system than we have. I remember the scripture where Paul spoke about being content with what you have, and it made a lot more sense to me. Even in a country where there is an abundance like in America, being content is still important. Remember that being content does not mean one stops believing. It simply means you are praising the Lord where you are right then.

Always strive for God's best: the best job, the best home, the best car. Our confusion at times can be compared with Israel. When God gave them manna in the desert, the Israelites complained, and when God showed them the honey and milk and the fruits from the promised land, they complained and said that they were unable to obtain and possess God's promises.

> And all these blessings shall come on thee, and overtake thee if thou shalt hearken unto the voice of the Lord thy God. . . . And the Lord shall command the blessings upon thee in thy storehouse, and in all that thou settest thine hand unto, and He shall bless thee in the land that the Lord thy God givest thee.
>
> Deuteronomy 28:2, 8

As God's children, we should always remember that we are not God's step children. God simply does not have any stepchildren. Just as Jesus was the only begotten son of God so through Christ Jesus all of us who have accepted His word become *sons of God.* Remember that God does not qualify His sons by gender either. Every one who believes becomes a s*on of God.* That qualifies you whether you are a man or a woman. God also calls the church the bride of Christ; you are part of the bride even when you are a man; it has nothing to do with gender.

Abraham's Cousin Johan in Africa!

> And the Lord said unto Abraham, after that Lot was separated from him, lift up now thine eyes, and look from the place where thou now art Northward, and Southward, and Eastward, and Westward. For all the land which thou seest, to thee will I give it, and to thy seed for ever.
>
> Genesis 13:14–15

Can God still give someone land today, like He gave to Abraham? Consider the fact that every piece of land on earth already belongs to someone. Could someone today actually cut a covenant with God?

I often wondered if there were any of God's people today who are actually walking in the blessings of God as it was promised to Israel in the Old Testament. That is until I met a man by the name of Johan Venter at a camp meeting where I was invited to be the evening speaker. Johan was a farmer in the Free State, a province of the republic of South Africa, near the town called Bethlehem. After the conference was over, Johan invited me and my family to spend a few days at his farm where he lived with his wife and five married sons. He told me that he operated his farm on the Blessings of Abraham, under the new covenant, which is a better covenant, and sealed with the blood of Jesus. He also told me that as the priest of his household, according to the Word of God, that as long as he lives according to God's word and obeyed the commandments of Christ, that he as God's child had the rights to the power of blessing of this covenant.

> But now hath He obtained a more excellent ministry, by how much He is the mediator of a better covenant, which was established upon better promises.
>
> Hebrews 8:6

Johan shared with me a little bit about his life story. "One day," he said, "my one son had a car accident, and died in the hospital. I was notified by the doctor, who I know me very well. I immediately got into my car and drove to the hospital; when I arrived there and wanted to see my son, the doctor and several nurses tried to stop me, because he was dead. They said there was nothing I could do for him. I pushed my way pass the doctor and the nurses and to the bed where my son was laying. They already had the curtain pulled around his bed, and had covered his face with a sheet. I pulled the sheet off, grabbed him by his shoulders and said as loud as I could, "Satan! You cannot take his life, he belongs to me!" Then I said to my son, "In the name of *Jesus,* get up let's go home!" Immediately my son lifted himself off the bed and stood to his feet. Johan said the doctor and nurses were standing there in amazement. The doctor suddenly called the nurses and told them to bring the man oxygen and told me to get out the room so they can give him medical treatment for his injuries. "But," says Johan, "I said doctor, you did not treat him when you had the chance, instead you let him die. No! You had your chance. Besides what can you do for him now after God gave him back to me?" Then we walked out of the hospital and went home.

Johan also told me that he started his farm with thirty acres. He was so poor at the time he got married, the only way he could afford to build himself a house was from rocks he gathered on the farm. But Johan had a covenant with God. He was fully persuaded that as long as he upheld his part of the covenant, that God would uphold His part of the covenant. That God did His part was obvious by the evidence that surrounded us. Johan asked me if I would like to see his farm. "Yes, I would." I replied. We took off in his truck and he and I drove across thousands of acres of the most beautiful farmland I have ever seen. Every inch of land in itself spoke of the abundance of God and reminded me of Abraham.

> And the Lord said unto Abram, after that Lot was separated from him, Lift up now thine eyes, and look from the place where thou now art Northward, and Southward, and Eastward, and Westward. For all the Land that thou seest, to thee will I give it, and to thy seed forever.
>
> Genesis 13:14–15

Wow! But that was then and now is now. Think of it; God can't do it any more, or can He?. For one, all the land already belongs to someone. It is not uninhabited like in the days of Abraham. Except no-one told Johan. As we were driving over mile after mile of farmland, Johan began to tell me how God was his partner. "I bought this land, one farm at a time, and I can travel forty miles in any direction and never leave my farm" he told me. While we were traveling on a graveled dirt road, which was in better shape than the county roads, on the way I counted over forty of the largest tractors I had ever seen, plowing mile after mile of farm land. We also passed many eighteen wheelers carrying grain; it was impossible to imagine such a large operation. I had never seen anything like that in my life. "Every thing you see belongs to me." Johan further explained.

Later when we got back to the house and were sitting down with a cup of coffee, Johan continued to tell me, he said, "Pastor Corrie, many years ago I made up my mind that I was going to live my life by God's covenant. I dedicated all I have to God. I reminded my children daily from the day they were born, that they are a chosen generation and a royal priesthood. I confess the Blessings of the covenant every day, and God has blessed me all these years. The more I listened to Johan telling me about his covenant with God, the more it sounded like a Bible story. I myself believe in faith. I have read all the faith books of Dr. Kenneth Hagin, Oral Roberts, Kenneth Copeland. However, what I was seeing was one man's faith in action who has never read any other faith book accept the Word of the Ever Living, Ever Lasting God of the universe. The same God who says in Matthew 5:18:

> For verily I say unto you, Till heaven and earth pass, one jot or one tittle shall in no wise pass from the law, till all be fulfilled.
>
> Matthew 5:18
>
> Jesus Christ the same yesterday and today and forever.
>
> Hebrews 13:8
>
> For I am the Lord, I change not; therefore ye sons of Jacob are not consumed.
>
> Malachi 3:6

Johan was convinced that God was still the same and obligated by His word to do the same for him in the twentieth century. Johan said, "Don't think that Satan has not tempted me with unbelief, because he has many times. One day we came home from church and a hailstorm came across our farm while we were at church. In my fields I could not see the wheat in my fields which was about two feet tall; all I could see was white hail. Usually the hail cuts the wheat off at ground level. My sons and I started walking across our fields and spoke to the wheat. We said, "Wheat, in Jesus name you will not be broken, but you will stand up and grow when the hail is melted." After we got back home I received phone calls from various farmers saying that their wheat was cut to the ground and all their wheat was lost. When they asked me about my wheat, I said to them, I am not concerned about my wheat, I expect my wheat to stand up after the sun had time to melt the ice. The result was, all the farmers got what they confessed they had and I got what I expected. After the ice melted my wheat all stood up tall, and because my neighbors crops were cut down by the hail, I sold mine for more money than I would have gotten if theirs did not fail. So you see the covenant works for me.

"There was another time when my sons came and called me, saying the Caterpillar worms covered my corn. I could run my hand up the stem of the corn and would have a hand full of worms. My sons and I began to walk the borders of my farm and commanded all the worms to leave my farm and die on the fences. The next day the worms were lying up to two feet on the fences, all dead. My neighbors lost all their corn and were paid out by insurance if they had any. I had a bumper crop and again I got very good prices for my corn. You see pastor," Johan said to me. "I don't have to carry insurance, because God is my insurance. I also don't use any pesticide on my lands, because God conditionally warrantees the outcome of my crops; neither do I have to use fertilizer. While I do my part, I have God's assurance that He will do His part. Believe it or not, I have the easy part."

Johan's love for God and training others to receive the kingdom of God was also evident by the schools on his farm. Johan's five daughters-in-law were all school teachers, and all were working in the farm schools that Johan had built for the children of the farm laborers. Usually the children of farm laborers have no opportunity to attend school, but not if Johan could help it. Buses left his farm early every morning to pick up children from neighboring farms. The school is free for all children who wish to attend Johan's private Christian School.

Every time a new child gets enrolled, the child also get fitted for a uniform for school. The child gets free meals, free medical attention if they need it. Best of all, the child doesn't only learn how to write and read. The child also learns about Jesus and how to walk and live in Christ.

Why am I telling you the story about Johan? Because when you live your life in God's economy, and conduct your life, your business, your problems, your enemies, according to the laws of the secret kingdom as seen in Matthew chapters five, six, seven and throughout the teachings of Jesus, you are living on a higher plane, and you fall under the laws of God's secret kingdom. His is the kingdom that has no end. God's kingdom, is the kingdom the world cannot see, but it is real. The only way we can live in it, is by choice. Yes it can feel lonely at times, and you may wonder how many other people are out there who are willing to trust God? Don't fear, they are out there, the question is, "are you?" God's army is always on the move. The question you may ask is, "Am I in that army?" I thought you were. I also thought you may enjoy hearing about other believers who walk by faith. Because

God's army stretches from country to country, and from sea to shining sea.

Although I was walking by faith and teaching the kind of faith Johan lived, I myself had never red a book on faith or heard any teaching on the subject until I came to Tulsa. I remember once listening to Kenneth Copeland teach and said to God. "This is amazing that you have revealed such spiritual insight to this man whom I had never heard of."

After Genny and I finished Bible School, God made it possible for me to purchase 10,000 of Dr. Kenneth Hagin's books and distribute them free in South Africa. A year later when I returned to the States I found several South Africans at Rhema Bible College as a direct result. After Bible School, Kenneth Copeland gave me 60 of his teaching tapes at no cost and permission to duplicate the tapes. Not only did I see people who got saved as a result, but we were able to duplicate and distribute many copies free of charge.

Manna From Heaven

And Jesus answered and said, verily I say unto you. There is no man that hath left house or brethren, or sisters, or father, or mother, or wife, or children, or lands, for my sake and the gospels, but he shall receive a hundredfold now in this time, houses and bretheren, and sisters, and mothers, and children and lands, with persecutions: and in the world to come eternal life.

Mark 10:29, 30

Genny and I had no time to sit around in our little roach invested trailer. I had a few engagements set up, and in a couple of days we had a revival in a small Arkansas town. While we were talking about the upcoming meetings, there came a unexpected knock on the door. I got up and opened the door. The lady at the door was one of the ladies who was at the women's retreat where Genny was a speaker just a week ago. She asked if she could come in; we invited her in and apologized for the trailer. She seemingly did not care and started to tell us that the Lord laid it on her heart to give us a check for thirty-five hundred dollars. We were pleasantly surprised to say the least. It was not that we were broke, I had not even touched the ten thousand dollars from the sale of the car. Neither was it that we didn't expect a miracle from God. Sure, we had been praying for miracles. I was praying for a miracle every day, just out of habit. I guess I was just surprised that someone would drive from Colorado to Oklahoma to give me some money. We thanked her and the Lord and moments later she was on her way. After the check had cleared the bank I thought just out of courtesy, that I owed it to the intern specialist to pay the two thousand dollars he billed me, in person, just in the event he wanted to know where the money came from, so I could tell him that God provided the money for my doctor bill.

We only stayed in the roach infested trailer for one month. I found a large double wide on the lake where we moved into the following month. The double wide was also very near to where the Bible College was where I was going to teach that following year, except at that moment we did not know that I was going to teach there. It was the last year that Trinity was open as a Bible College. Dr. Duncome who was the founder of Trinity, where Genny and I attended, had already decided to retire.

The property on which the College was situated belonged to another organization called International faith. While Genny and the children were still in South Africa, I had a invitation to preach at the church which was pastored by the president of this organization. The attendance was extremely small that Sunday night, the total number of people there was twelve, that in it self may not have had any significance, except for the fact that during that service God gave me a word of knowledge for everyone of the twelve people who was there except for the pastor. When God gives me as the preacher a word of knowledge for individuals in such a small setting, I realize how very vulnerable I become, because in such a small setting every body knows the ins and outs of everyone who's present. That means, you as the preacher or the prophet have to have heard from God, or you can get yourself in some serious trouble. For that reason I make sure that I spend serious prayer time with the Lord before each service. In this instance, God gave me a word for each of eleven people excluding the pastor.

After the service the pastor invited me to his house for coffee. While at his home he called me to his office and said, "I know every one of those people who you gave a message to from the Lord, I can also tell you that every word of every message, addressed exactly the problems each of those people struggles with right now. What I don't understand is why God had nothing for me?" I said, "Pastor, I don't know either why God gave me nothing for you, except the Lord is giving me a word for you right now as we speak. The Lord says for me to tell you that He has made it known to you that He wishes for you to re-open the Bible College that was discontinued by Dr. Duncome. Are you willing to do that?" The pastor acted like he was not surprised at all; in fact he said to me, "Brother Corrie that's exactly the confirmation I wanted from the Lord." He opened the drawer of his desk and pulled out an envelope out of which he pulled a letter and said to me, "Read this." The letter was from a man in Canada who claims to be a prophet of God. As I read the letter I saw that this prophet was saying to the pastor, "God is showing me that there is a Bible College he wants you to continue. If you're not sure that's what God wants you to do, wait, because he will send someone else to confirm what I am telling you."

Is God really concerned about our affairs, so much so that he will confirm prayers or even judge our deeds? Explore with me what happened in the early church and decide for your self.

Ananias and Sapphira, are two members of Peter's church. They decide to make a hefty donation to the church, except they kind of twist the truth just a little. They decide to tell the church that they were giving all the proceeds from the sale of their property, when in fact they kept some of the proceeds for themselves. Big deal? Yes, indeed, the early church thought that not telling the truth was a big deal. Ananias was already dead when his wife came in and confirmed what her husband had said.

> And Peter answered unto her, Tell me whether you sold the land for so much? and she said yea, for so much. Then Peter said unto her, How is it that ye have agreed together to tempt the Spirit of the Lord? behold, the feet of them which have buried thy husband are at the door, and shall carry thee out. Then fell she down straight way at his feet, and yielded up the ghost; and the young men came in, and found her dead, and carrying her forth, buried her by her husband.
>
> Acts 5:8–10

Please note that the sin was not that they kept some of the money for themselves. The money was already theirs to do with as they pleased. What was wrong was the fact that they had lied about it Today we live in a society where concealing the truth, or revealing the true facts are not always considered relevant. But speaking the truth in God's eyes is still considered serious business. Look at what God's word says about lying,

"But the fearful, and the unbelieving, and the abominable, and murderers, and whoremongers, and all liars, shall have their part in the lake which burneth with fire and brimstone; which is the second death" Revelation 21:8.

Yes! I believe that scripture supports the theory that God really and truly desires to interact with His beloved children, if only we would afford Him the time. God interacted with Elijah who was fed by ravens twice daily, "And the Ravens brought him bread and flesh in the morning, and bread and flesh in the evening, and he drank of the brook" (1 Kings 17:6).

I think as God's children that the worst mistake we make is to think God is not watching and he does not really care. At one time I thought that I could do things and God wouldn't care, until the Holy Spirit renewed my thinking. Now I realize that I can talk to Jesus all the time, in the car driving, lying in bed, where ever, the Holy Spirit is right there where we are. Paul tells us to put off doubtful or negative thinking and realize that He is always with us.

> But that isn't the way Christ taught you! If you have already heard His voice and learned from Him the truths concerning Himself, Then throw off your old evil nature - the old you that was a partner in your evil ways - rotten through and through, full of lust and sham. Now your attitudes and thoughts must all be changing for the better.
>
> Ephesians 4:20–23, TLB

The amplified says it like this: "And be constantly renewed in the spirit of your mind-having a fresh mental and spiritual attitude" (Ephesians 4:23, AMP).

God is watching your every move, every moment of every day, and waiting and willing to take you as a partner if you will only let Him. Tune Him in, ask for guidance, be consistently aware of his presence, obey the Spirit, ask for direction. With God as a partner on your side, you will see your life change for the better.

The day we moved into our new double wide trailer was on a Sunday morning. We stopped by the trailer on our way to the church where I was to preach that morning. I did not know anyone at that church. I had not even met the pastor before and did not want to get to the church with a car load of luggage. What we had in the car was the luggage we came to the United States with. We basically just emptied the trunk of the car and unloaded everything we owned on the floor of the mobile home. After a full day of ministering to new people we had never met before, we were all very tired and ready for bed when we got back to our new home around 11:30 PM. As I entered the door, I turned on the light and my first thought was that in the dark we entered the wrong trailer. As I looked around I saw a beautifully furnished home. I said, "Genny! this is the wrong house, this is not our place. Let's get out of here." She said, "It can't be, this is the right place." She usually takes a lot more notice of details than I do. I went back outside to take another look just to be sure. From everything I remembered it was the right trailer. While I was still standing in the door way, Genny had pushed her way passed me and went inside the trailer. I whispered loudly, "You better get out of there, you will wake the people inside." Then she replied quite loud, "This is our trailer, and someone has furnished it!" "That can't be possible, who could have furnished it?" I replied. But Genny found a note that read as follows, "Don't be too surprised, the furniture is from God to the Joubert family." No name or any other explanation was given.

After the initial shock, we started to take a good look in order to evaluate what had been given. Most of the furniture was really good expensive furniture, the beds were all made with linens and pillows on, in the bathrooms were towels and toiletries, in the kitchen were pots and pans, dishes, cups, silverware, a refrigerator The only thing we had two of was toasters. We were fully out fitted, all four bedrooms, the dining room, lounge and den from one end of the house to the other end of the house. Let me say this, if you have never experienced anything like this, to say the least, it is a very humbling experience. I did not know if I should cry or laugh. To figure God's participation in my life has always been very joyful for me. With tears in my eyes, I could think of nothing else to say than just, "Thank you Jesus." What can one say to a Friend that even furnishes your house while you are gone.

One thing I have found is that God keeps his word. The Lord reminded me again of the scripture in Matthew 10:9–10: "Provide neither gold, nor silver, nor brass in your purses, nor script for your journey, neither two coats, neither shoes nor yet stave's, for the workman is worthy of his meat."

You may ask, will God do this for me? Probably not; in my experience God does not make carbon copies. He will treat each person according to their circumstances as He sees fit.

In the ministry, I have experienced both good times and bad times. Abundance at times and very lean days at other times. But all in all, God has always brought us through. In the ministry, I have also worked with sheep, and I have worked with wolves in sheep's clothing.

The real test for me came a few days afterwards, when the Lord said to me that I should offer my assistance to teach at the new Bible College, and to offer to teach for free, not to accept any money. Now I had done a lot of things up till now, but working for no money, that I had not done before. I reminded God just to be sure He understood, that I had a wife and four children to support. Well off cause he already knew it, but I was still a human living in a human body, with human fears. However, in obedience I did as God had instructed me, and I was accepted for a teaching position on the spot. The summer holidays were over now and it was just about time for school to start back up. It was the end of the summer of 1975, a summer I won't easily forget. I had only been back in the United States since the end of May, and so many things already happened, I could have written a book. I also had to get my own children in school, and wondered how they would compete in a society so vastly different than the one we came from. My first challenge came when I enrolled my eldest daughter Virginia into school. Back in South Africa she would have started in the 10th grade.

Here I was sitting with her in the principal's office and he was telling me that in his opinion, Virginia had a disadvantage being from another country. Even though she was fully bilingual and fluent in English, the school principal suggested she be enrolled in the ninth grade. Virginia looked at me and as I looked at her I could see her total disgust. I knew she was smart, but as the principal said she also needed credits which she did not have and could not have brought with her from overseas. I could see out the corner of my eye that Virginia was looking at me with pleading eyes that were saying, "No please, don't let me start in the ninth grade." The principal was looking at me, it was my turn to talk. I said, "Could you give her a chance? I know that she would have to work extra hard, but if you could start her in the tenth grade and if in six weeks her work is not up to par, we will put her in the ninth grade?" The principal agreed. All our children went to the next grades and together we made a covenant with God to pray every single morning and ask God to help them. Since I was the one to take them to school, I would hold their hands just before they got out of the car and let them repeat with me:

Philippians 4:13, "I can do all things through Christ who strengtheneth me-"

Also the second part of Mark 9:23-"all things are possible to him that believeth."

After we confessed these scriptures together, I would say to them, "Repeat after me, I can do whatever school work is given to me today, because Christ is in me." They would repeat after me and then run off to school. I believe my two girls took to heart the efforts I made, and the instruction I gave them, not once, not twice, but day after day for all the years they were at school. How did God respond to our prayers and confessions? Was all that effort worth it? My answer, yes it was; both my girls had enough credits and both graduated out of the eleventh grade and went on to College. Think for a moment: in all honesty, who does God's word say the devil is? God's word says that the devil is a liar and the truth is not in him. When the school principal said that they could not do it in the normal time, that it would be impossible, may have been true in the normal sense, but we should excel or lift ourselves out of what is normal. The scripture says,

> But ye are a chosen generation, a royal priesthood, and a holy nation, a peculiar people, that ye should show forth the praises of Him, who hath called you out of darkness into His marvelous light.
>
> 1 Peter 2:9

How else will the world know who we are if they can't see that there is a difference between us and them? They should come to the realization that there is a higher power at work in us, or they won't believe. We as believers also have to live by a higher standard, because in us and for us works that higher power.

Jesus said: "If ye hath faith as a grain of mustard seed, ye shall say unto this mountain, remove hence to yonder place, and it shall remove, and nothing shall be impossible unto you" (Matthew 17:20).

Well, Virginia and Gillian both completed their grades with time left to spare. Why? I think they believed that they could do it and they both did.

God did something else, very remarkable, for them. Both

Virginia and Gillian developed testimonies while they were students. I would like to tell you about Virginia first. While in College during her first year she became the leader of the foreign students, and used every opportunity to bring someone home with her. She also stood up for her beliefs and principles, which she would not compromise. After leading an Iranian girl who was some kind of priest in the Moslem faith, to Christ Jesus, some students from the foreign student body summoned her to the library and confronted her for leading this Iranian Girl to Christ. That, however, did not deter her or her new Christian friend; both stood firmly for what they believed in. Today she continues her ministry as the Holy Spirit leads her.

Our second daughter Gillian came to us when she was in the eleventh grade one day. She told us that she was one of two girls who had worked through all the competition to become president for the student body, which ended in a tie. To break the tie it was decided that they should both wear mini dresses to school the next day, and each give a speech. She said that she did not think that she should have to wear a mini dress and wanted our opinion.

Genny and I both encouraged her not to lower her principles, because God will use her in some other way if she was not chosen. The following day at school when she gave her speech, she told the student body that she was not prepared to lower her standards in order to win the election, because she was a Christian, and that she did not feel that the Lord would be proud of her if she wore a mini dress. But, she told them if she was chosen, she would serve the student body to the best of her abilities. Well, she did not win the election, but God gave her something far greater. That same day after she got home from school, the phone rang, it was one of the high school football players. The boy told Gillian that her courage to speak out and not be ashamed of the Lord really meant a lot to him. He also told Gillian of family problems at home that was more than he was able to deal with. Gillian suggested that she could pray with him if he wanted her to. He said he would like for her to pray with him, and they prayed over the phone. During the following weeks, more and more students were calling Gillian for counsel on the phone and eventually some of the students organized a before school prayer meeting with Gillian in the lead. As the days and weeks passed Genny and I often found her sitting in her room with the phone on the floor in a corner in her bedroom with tears streaming down her face while talking to a fellow student about the Lord.

God always gives his children the best end of the deal. Not only did Gillian win a victory over old Satan, but in the process God also gave her souls with eternal rewards.

> The wolf also shall dwell with the lamb, and the leopard shall lie down with the kid; and the calf and the young lion and the fatling together; and a little child shall lead them.
>
> Isaiah 11:6

> Train up a child in the way he should go, and when he is old, he will not depart from it.
>
> Proverbs 22:6

> Withhold not correction from the child, for if thou beatest him with a rod, he shall not die.
>
> Proverbs 23:13

Children will follow the examples set by their families.

Unfortunately too many of our children will be lost because they had no real God fearing role model to look up to.

Trouble in the Secret Kingdom

> And a vision appeared to Paul in the night; There stood a man of Macedonia, and prayed him, saying, Come over into Macedonia and help us.
>
> Acts 16:9

I was enjoying my work at the Bible College during the early seventies as Professor of church history and Old Testament studies. I also enjoyed our students who were working hard, eager to learn God's word. To me it is refreshing to find young people who, despite all the distractions of the world, still want to learn about God's alternatives. Usually my weekends were booked with speaking somewhere at a church or fellowship. These appointments along with my job at the Bible College, kept me fully occupied.

We were living in a double wide trailer which was sitting only about fifty feet from the lake's water front, where my family and I spent many pleasant evenings sitting on the side of the water in the hot humid air of Oklahoma, while our twin boys were fishing, and our two girls perhaps swimming.

One morning after our children had already left for school, My wife Genny and I were sitting at the breakfast table just chatting, when she told me about a dream she had that night.

Neither of us placed too much emphasis on dreams. Both of us were well aware that the enemy had used dreams in the past that were not from God to instill fear or confusion, or that one could just be dreaming with no meaning which is natural. On the other hand, I didn't want to make light of the dream either. I wanted to be open, if for any reason the Holy Spirit was using the dream as a communication tool to us, which of course is perfectly scriptural. The apostle Peter quoted this scripture from an Old Testament prophesy found in Joel 2:28, "And it shall come to pass in the last days saith God, I will pour my Spirit upon all flesh: and your sons and your daughters shall prophesy, and your young men shall see visions, and your old men shall dream dreams" (Acts 2:17).

The dream was a tool often used by the Holy Spirit to communicate God's answer to men in the Old Testament. One of the most favorite of such occurrences was the dream of Pharaoh, for which God gave the interpretation to Joseph.

> Then it came to pass at the end of two full years, that Pharaoh had a dream; and behold, he stood by the river. Suddenly there came up out of the river seven cows, fine looking and fat; and they fed in the meadow. Then behold seven other cows came up after them out of the river, ugly and gaunt, and stood by the other cows on the bank of the river. And the ugly and gaunt cows ate up the seven fine looking and fat cows. So Pharaoh awoke.
>
> Geneses 42:1–7, NKJV

To the king the dream was not only puzzling, but it bothered him so much that he called all his advisors to see if there was anyone who was able to interpret his dream. The Bible further tells us that after the king exhausted all his resources of likely information, then someone told him about Joseph.

It is noteworthy to realize that even though Joseph at this point of his life had been unfairly treated, serving a prison sentence for something he was totally innocent of. That Joseph maintained what every child of God should maintain, an ongoing relationship with God despite the circumstances.

Imagine, being imprisoned, serving year after year for something you are not even guilty of. Will you blame God for your calamity? Will you stop serving Him? Will you stay in a continual depression, or will you continue to praise Him regardless of the surrounding circumstances?

Now notice that someone tells the king that there is a prisoner who they knew could interpret his dream. "Then Pharaoh sent and called Joseph, and they brought him hastily out of the dungeon; and he shaved, changed his clothing, and came to Pharaoh" (Genesis 41:14, NKJV).

After Joseph heard the dream of the king, Joseph was quick to tell the King that he himself did not possess the power to interpret dreams, but that he relied on God for the interpretation. More important is the fact that years of abuse, living in the dungeon had not bittered Joseph who was still on talking terms with God. Joseph was still praying, still being led by the spirit.

Never think that God does not know where you are or what you are doing. At times we feel that God should have answered our prayer yesterday already. But remember He is God; we don't order Him around or give Him a time frame to perform in. All He promised you and me is that when you ask, He will answer you. The secret is not to waver, but to stand firm in your faith, because He who promised you can not lie. "Let us hold fast to the confession of our hope without wavering, for He who promised is faithful" (Hebrews 10:23, NKJV).

Genny said that in her dream she saw three men from a large church who were waiving, like they were beckoning me to come to them up north. She said that she knew in her spirit that they were not calling her, but that they were calling me to come and help them. Genny also said she did not know which city they were from. The whole thing sounded very strange, but there was something else there, like a spiritual mystique. I don't know if you ever felt this, but I had often said that working for God is no less adventuresome than being a "James Bond." Yes! I know someone may take exception to me saying this, but in my walk with the Lord I have never found my work boring. In fact, if one walks in the Spirit, the excitement begins when the gifts begin to operate, and God begins to deal with people, and the Holy Spirit begins to reveal hidden secrets of the heart; healings take place and relationships get restored. At other times God speaks in secret codes where the information comes in bits and pieces, but eventually you will get the whole picture.

Once I was ministering at a small country church, where I knew absolutely no one. After the meeting was already in progress for about ten minutes, the Spirit of the Lord said to me, "Do you see what is happening here?" I said, "No. What is happening here Lord?" Often when one is a speaker in a small church, and if that speaker is from overseas, people in the church put on their best show. Here they were doing it also, except here were two groups, first the one group sings with their pianist, and then the next group sings with their pianist. I did not think anything was out of the ordinary. Next the Spirit of the Lord said to me, "Call the two piano players to the front so you can pray for them and ask them to hold hands." When the music and singing finished I did as the Spirit told me to do and called the two piano players to the front, with no idea why I was doing what I was doing. The two ladies came to the front, and I said, "The Lord wants me to pray for you." They were standing one on the one side of the podium and the other one on the other side of the podium about ten feet apart. The Spirit of the Lord then said to me, "Tell them you want them to hold hands when you pray for them."

I asked the two piano players to move closer together and to hold hands. I then asked the church to also hold hands, but I asked them to stretch across the isle holding hands. Nothing happened, no one moved, I thought maybe they did not hear me. I asked everyone again, the church and the two musicians to move closer and to hold hands, but no one stirred. The people in the pews were holding hands, but they did not stretch their hands across the aisle as the Lord told me they were supposed too. Now on the surface nothing seemed so wrong, but the Spirit was about to unveil the secrets of their hearts. The Spirit said, "You go down there to them, take the two piano players by the hand, bring them together and you place their hands into each others hands and pray for them." That in itself is no "biggie." I don't know why they were reluctant, so I walked to where they were to help them. I took the first lady by the hand and start pulling on her, and said, "Come with me."

We walked to where the other lady was standing and just as I got ready to take her by the hand also, the Spirit said, "Tell them that the Lord loves them both and that they should hug each other." Suddenly it sounded like a dam wall that had burst! Crying and tears, and apologies, not only by the two piano players, but all across the church, they were crying and hugging and asking forgiveness from one another. I was standing there totally dumbfounded. I still did not have the slightest idea what was going on. Except for one thing, I had no control, I think I could have walked out of that church and no one would have noticed. Not that I would have, no sir, I wanted to see what was happening and I was just waiting for things to calm down enough so I could find out. No this was too much fun to miss one second of it. Have you ever noticed how much fun church becomes when the Holy Spirit starts moving?

After things quieted down a little, one of the elders came to the front and asked everyone to sit down, then turned to me and began to tell me how a rift had began to develop in the church over the stretch of about two years. It all started when one of the piano players in the church got divorced. Some of the members in the church accepted her divorce, and was willing to forgive her and to continue to love her. However, others felt condemnation towards her that she could no longer minister in music because of her divorce. The church became divided after months of bickering, and tensions between the two sides grew. One half of the church would not participate when she played. The other half of the church got their own piano player. However, while all this bickering was beginning to get out of hand, some in the church had started to pray for God to bring unity and restoration back to their church. But today, disguised as a preacher, the Holy Spirit called in a Secret Agent, working as a preacher in God's invisible kingdom of light, to expose the dark works of the invisible kingdom of God's enemy "Satan," and in the exposition the Holy Spirit was able to restore peace and unity. All I did was to follow directions. The Holy Spirit was the one that did the restoration and healing of old wounds.

Well, I just wanted to throw in that little extra information. It really is exciting to be one of God's secret agents on assignment to bust open Satan's cesspool of contempt towards God's people and sent the demons scattering out of there, so to speak, "with their tails on fire." I wished that I could have seen the devils that oppressed that church. I wished I could have seen them hurry and scurry out of that church, as the Holy Ghost was lighting the fire under their tails.

Now let me take you back to my story about Genny's dream. About 5 PM. that same evening of the morning Genny woke up and told me her dream. We were just sitting down to dinner when the phone rang. The voice on the other side was that of the F.G.B.M.F.I. chapter president of St. Paul Minneapolis. He said they were looking for a speaker in two weeks. He also said the speaker they originally booked for that night had to cancel. He wanted to know if I could accept to be their speaker at such short notice. I did not know if I could, I told him I had a speaking engagement already made for that night, but that I would pray about it and call him back.

As soon as I hung up the phone, Genny reminded me about her dream. Genny said to me, "Do you think that this unexpected phone call could have anything to do with the dream I had last night?" I said, "Well Honey, I don't really know what to think. That phone call and your dream about the church up north with the three men asking me to help them seems just a little bit too coincidental; what do you think?" "St. Paul is about as north as one can get from Tulsa." Genny replied. "Furthermore, I suggest we pray and ask the Lord." Well, that sounded good to me. The two of us found ourselves a private place and began to pray, asking the Lord what I was supposed to do. After we got through praying we both felt the same witness in our spirits that I should cancel everything else and go to St. Paul Minneapolis. When I returned the chapter president's call, I mentioned to him why I felt that it was important for me to go to their chapter. I said to him, "I feel that maybe God wanted to use the F.G.B.M.F.I. meeting as a stepping stone for me to meet the three men in Genny's dream." He had no comment and was not aware of a connection if there was anything.

Two weeks later someone from the F.G.B.M.F.I. chapter was at the airport to meet me, "God's secret agent." Except no one knew who I really was, or why exactly I was there. I was there disguised as the speaker for the F.G.B.M.F.I. The usual practice at these chapters is to gather together a few men before the meeting starts to pray with and lay hands on the speaker. After the men finished praying for me, the president of the chapter suggested that I share Genny's dream with the prayer circle of men. After I shared the dream, everyone started to leave for their seats, except three men who walked up to me, [The three men in Genny's dream]. The one said, "Brother, the three of us are the senior elders of a large church in the city. Our pastor was recently relieved from his pastoral duties because of sin which he had committed and confessed to the board. The church board felt that it would best serve the church if he left, but our church is in a grieving process. The pastor was a good man and he has built the church and a large Bible College. What makes this so sad is that everyone loved him. Since he left the church, we have been praying that God would send someone to minister healing to our congregation, and we feel God has sent you. Will you preach for us tomorrow?"

Sunday morning in this church there were well over a thousand people in the service. But even before the service, early that Sunday morning, God began to deal with me about immorality and broken homes. The three elders did not tell me what the sin was that the pastor committed and I did not ask either. I found out later that the Pastor had a affair with a member of the church. From experience I have learned the less I know the better. If God chose to deal with it through me, I would deal with it, and for that reason I never need to know anything in advance. The outcome of that meeting resulted in me staying for four additional days counseling and praying with individuals who got hurt in the process of their pastors misconduct.

Today more than ever before, we need Christians who are

strong in the word of God. We also need more than ever to learn to walk in the spirit. Our churches need the five fold ministry for protection. Too often have we seen great ministries build on the efforts and hard work of one personality, who after years of commitment to that ministry, falls into a trap set by Satan. They didn't fall because they did not know God's word. But rather because they did not submit themselves any longer to His word and the shared authority of the five fold ministry.

The saying still rings true today: It's not how well you start out, or how much you accomplish, but it is how well you finish out that counts. If only we can hear the word of Jesus again, and let it sink into our spirit. Listen again to these words spoken by our Savior, "For what is a man profited, if he shall gain the whole world, and lose his soul? Or what shall a man give in exchange for his soul?" (Matthew 16:26).

When one lives in a society like the one we all live in today, Christians need to be stronger and more careful than ever. Edwin Louis Cole in his book "Strong Men in Tough Times" is speaking to men when he writes, "What is submitted grows stronger. What is resisted grows weaker." That is not only true for men, but for every child of God.

In my experience in walking with God, I have found that people who live their lives by the principles of the sermon on the mount, are the ones who are building on a solid foundation. Dr. Pat Robertson in his book "The Secret Kingdom," says this to the church: Our problem has been with the word *meek* in the King James Version. It does mean "humble" and "gentle," even "docile." But the definition cannot stop there. Biblical meekness does not call for abject surrender of one's character or personal integrity. It calls for a total yielding of the reins of life from one's own hands. But it does not stop there either. The meek exercise discipline, which results in their being kept continuously under

God's control." You may well ask yourself this question, who is in control of me, my life, my actions? Is *Jesus* your Lord and Commander in charge of your life? Are you pushing forward, closer, seeking, yielding, doing, giving? Give what He asks, do what He commanded, take what He gives you? He asks for your Life, He gave you salvation. Surrendering to His command will keep you focused on Him. He commands you to be a soul winner, one who actively participates in helping the Father to build the family business. Many Christians fall short because they are waiting for someone to hold their hand. Remember these powerful words of Jesus.

> And from the days of John the Baptist until the present time the kingdom of heaven has endured violent assault, and violent men seize it by force [as a precious prize]-a share in the heavenly kingdom is sought for with the most ardent zeal and intense exertion.
>
> Matthew 11:12 AMP

In another quotation from Dr. Robertson's book, he states the following, "Though weaklings and wimps will fall by the wayside, God's meek men and women will inherit the earth." Considering the fact the power of God and the gifts of the Holy Spirit belong freely to every child who has accepted Jesus as their Lord, we all need to ask ourselves daily, "What have I done in the service of my Lord today?"

If you look back at your day and your answer is "nothing"; if your day passed and you are unable to recall anything you had done for God; you may want to analyze events and critique yourself to evaluate lost opportunities. Being effective as a disciple in the Lord's service does not revolve around preaching, or going to church or going to Bible study groups. Consider a kind word to someone at work, as being a disciple, or a prayer for someone, or directing someone to go to God in prayer. Often people are a lot more open than what is generally realized. Kindness in a kindless world goes a long way in the Lord's service. Jesus himself said this,

> He who receiveth you receiveth me, and he that receiveth me receive Him that send me. He that receiveth a prophet in the name of a prophet shall receive a prophets reward and he that receiveth a righteous man shall receiveth a righteous mans reward. And whosoever shall give to drink to these little ones a cup of cold water only in the name of a disciple, verily I say unto you, he shall in no wise lose his reward.
>
> Matthew 10:40–42

God Has More for You

> Therefore I say unto you, take no thought for your life, what ye shall eat, or what ye shall drink, nor yet for your body, what ye shall put on. Is not the life more than meat, and the body more than raiment? Behold the fowls of the air, for they sow not, neither do they reap, nor gather into barns; yet your heavenly father feedeth them all. Are ye not much better than they?
>
> Matthew 6:25, 26

Since our coming to the USA God has been very good to us. Even though we only had forty pounds of luggage each, when we came to America, God has since fully furnished our house for us. And even though I was teaching at the Bible College, receiving no pay check, God had met our needs in full every month. We, meaning Genny, the children and I, had not lacked in any thing. Yet even though Jesus plainly told us in the Bible, that we are important to God, and that He will take care of us, one realizes that to step out in faith is like taking a step into the unknown. It is not that one thinks that God won't perform His word, but I think perhaps it is more of a question of, how will God perform His word. I think some of us and perhaps most of us have heard about someone, perhaps a missionary or a friend, who had stepped out in faith and experienced horrendous hardship. I am not going to try and tell you why I think that occurs. The truth is I don't know, because I was not there. But I can tell you of my own experiences and I don't have any complaints about the way God has come through for me. Certainly walking by faith is an uncertainty due to the fact that you don't always know from day to day what is waiting for you. I won't encourage anyone to foolishly try to walk by faith. If one knows that God is calling you to take such a step, then do it by all means. But please make sure God is in it.

First, I believe, if anyone is going to try and walk by faith, they should be totally sold out to God. They should also know without a shadow of a doubt, that it is God that has called them to step out in faith. Secondly, it will help to have a prayer partner. Someone that can be in one accord with you. It is easier when someone agrees with you, than to be totally by one self. Genny and I are praying partners, and we both try to witness to what the Spirit is saying, especially when it involves major decisions. The Bible also teaches us that there is power in numbers, which is true even in one's spirit life. "Again I say unto you, that if two shall agree on earth as touching anything that they shall ask, it shall be done for them of my Father which are in heaven" (Matthew 18:19).

Praying for a Miracle House

Genny and I had been praying for a house, the double wide trailer was OK, but I needed more space and I needed an office. One morning while we were praying, the Lord said to me, "Go and find a house, once you found what you want, you can come back and tell me what you found." I told Genny and she said her spirit witnessed that is what we should do. It was one of my days off and I had no class to teach at the Bible College that day. I started to look in the phone book for a Realtor, once I found one I called him and set up a time to meet. I had no idea how purchasing a house in the States would work, but I thought if I get a Realtor, they would certainly guide me. After meeting with the Realtor he wanted to know what price range I had in mind. Since I had no knowledge of the market prices and absolutely no idea of how much money God would allow me. When I met with the Realtor, I suggested he show us houses in different price brackets so I could see what was available.

After driving around for half the day looking at houses he took us to a older house in a very nice and quiet neighborhood. The house was just the size we were looking for, freshly painted, it had a nice yard and an outside office. I think both Genny and I fell in love with the house the minute we saw it. I also felt that God would approve of my choice. Like the story of Goldie Locks and the Three Bears, not too big not too small but just right. So I said to the Realtor, "This is the house we want." He took us back to his office and said to us, "Do you want a loan or are you buying cash?" I could not tell him that I was actually only getting information to take back to God and had no idea what God had in mind. So I said, "We have not decided, but if you tell us what our chance is of getting a loan, then we will talk it over and get back with you." It only took him a few seconds to disqualify us for any loan. No credit history in the USA, no income history, full-time job with the College, but no salary and to crown it all a foreigner. "No," he said very emphatically, "you have no chance in getting a loan from any bank." I am afraid you would have to pay cash for the house if you want it. After Genny and I went home, we got onto our knees and we gave God the facts just like the Realtor gave it to us.

Now keep in mind that this entire house hunting venture was solely between God and us, no one else knew anything about it, that's no one except the Realtor. However, that evening I had a unexpected visitor, Dr. Duffy. I had not seen him in a while, and he had certainly never visited me before. I invited him in and asked him to what do we owe the pleasure of his company. He said he had heard that we were in town looking for a house. I wanted to know how he knew. Take in consideration that Tulsa even back in the early seventies had a population of a quarter million people. All he would say was that someone told him, but could not say who. It certainly was not that we wanted to keep the purchase of the house a secret. Rather, I just did not want to make a fool of myself. I preferred to keep certain things just between God and me. Next, Dr. Duffy wanted me to tell him where the house was. I told him where the house was, and I also told him we are still talking about it and have not made a final decision. But apparently Dr. Duffy did not hear me, because he began to tell us which schools our children would have to attend, as if it was a done deal. After about ten minutes he excused himself and said that he had to go, but wanted to know who the Realtor was that was handling the house for us, he said that he could check the price, just to make sure we get a good deal and don't get ripped off. I looked for the information and told him who the Realtor was and gave him the phone number.

It was three days later, nothing much had happened and Genny and I were still waiting on God to find out what He wanted us to do about the house. But that day we received a unexpected phone call. The man on the other side of the line was the real estate agent. My first thought was that he was calling to see if we had come to any decision yet. After we greeted he said, "I am just calling to congratulate you on your new home, and to tell you that the house will be yours to move into in thirty days." I stood there totally stunned, wondering if it's a prank, or if he was calling the wrong person. I said, "Excuse me, but what are you talking about?" He said again, "The house you and your wife looked at, all the paperwork has been taken care of, the house is yours." I said, "You must be mistaken, I have not signed any paperwork on the house." At which he replied, "Your friend took care of everything, did he not tell you?" I said, "No, I have no idea who the friend is you are talking about?" He started to laugh, and said, "You mean Dr. Duffy did not say anything to you? He came into my office the next morning after you and Mrs. Joubert looked at the house and asked me to show him the house you were interested in. When we got back to my office, he told me to have the paperwork ready by that evening. I did as he asked me and by that evening he came in and signed the contract. The house is yours Reverend Joubert. I thought your friend already told you. When I called him this morning to tell him the paperwork has been approved, he asked me to let you know which day you can move in." Stunned, I had to get a chair and just sit down for a while, I did not know if I should cry or laugh. All I could say was thank you Jesus, you are truly amazing. Did you ever feel so happy you could cry? When God told us in South Africa to sell everything and what we don't sell, just give away, we did it reluctantly and then there was Genny's list of things, which she thought God would not mind if she had someone store it for her. And the next day we got a phone call to say it all got stolen. And then something like this happens. I felt ashamed that at times I wondered if God really even cares. God just up and gave me a house. For a moment I think I felt what Peter must have felt after he denied Jesus three times.

I am so glad God does not deal with us as harshly as He did with the children of Israel, when they did not have enough faith to possess the promised land. But all the same, I do believe that each one of us have our own grace period in which we mature as the sons and the daughters of the Eternal King, and partakers of His splendid illustrious Glory. The Bible tells us, "That he might present it to himself a glorious church, not having spot or wrinkle, or any such thing, but that it will be holy and without blemish" (Ephesians 5:27).

Perhaps as Christian's we should pay more attention to these words when Jesus spoke to his disciples, and to us, "Then said Jesus unto his disciples, If any man will come after me, let him deny himself, and take up his cross, and follow me" (Matthew 16:24).

On the surface it might seem that our Lord is very demanding of His followers, and that life in Christ may cause undue suffering. But was that really what Jesus had in mind? No! I don't think so, because if suffering was intended as a condition of servitude, than Jesus would not have said,

> Come unto me, all ye that labor and are heavy laden, and I will give you rest. Take my yoke upon you, and learn of me; for I am meek and lowly in heart: and ye shall find rest upon your souls. For my yoke is easy, and my burden is light."
>
> Matthew 12:28–30

Or where it says in John 15:11, about receiving His joy in my life. I think Jesus is asking for total surrender of self, and total commitment to God. We as the church must be willing to commit totally to the guidelines Jesus gives us in the sermon on the mount Matthew chapters 5, 6, 7, and follow in His footsteps. Until we are sold out, and committed to live our lives and conduct our selves as God has commanded, we as a church will not enter into or experience the "Blessings" given to us in the New Testament promises either. God wants you and me to be able to experience His love. He wants us to know that even in a chaotic world as the one we are living in, that He can be our provider. He wants you to have a good job. He wants you to be successful. He wants you to walk in good health. He wants to put food on your table. You do not have to be in some kind of a full-time ministry to experience God's miraculous intervention into your life.

Has God called you? Yes! Yes! Jesus called you, He called all of us. I feel that every truly born again believer will feel the burden placed on them by the Holy Spirit compelling them to be effective in some form of a ministry. But you say, "I have a fulltime job!" All the better, full-time ministry does not mean preaching on Sundays, rather, it is to live your life a living testimony and render service to your neighbor.

Jesus paid my debt on Calvary's cross. Jesus purchased my release from Satan's enslavement. That is why, in my new life there is no basis for that, "feel sorry for one self attitude." That worthless grasshopper feeling that robbed Israel from receiving their inheritance and wants to prevent you from receiving all God has for you. Now I have the opportunity to exercise my free will and submit my life to the guidelines Jesus gave me in Matthew five, six, and seven. Read these chapters and study them. Compare what Jesus is saying by reading different translation. Matthew 5, 6, and 7, is the operations manual Jesus gave us. Jesus is saying, "If you follow these instructions, you will always please the Father.

You will be building on a solid foundation, or you will become fertile soil for God's word to grow in you and prosper you. The guidelines in Matthew 5, 6, and 7, was given to us to safeguard us and protect us. By following these guidelines we will not fall into Satan's captivity again. By strictly adhering to the guidelines in the owners operations manual, I began to bear fruit. While I continue in this fruit bearing process, my Father takes great pride in me. He waters me and fertilize me [providing all my needs according to his riches]. Never be hasty and expect God to jump to your demands. Anyone who has ever planted a fruit tree knows that the tree is not going to bear bushels of fruit in the first year. In fact it takes several years and a lot of pruning and watering before you are going to pick your first bushel, so be patient. Nature is God's timetable, in it we see the process which is also the same process that God uses in the spiritual realm.

Every believer following Jesus will encounter sometime in their life a compelling intervention. By that I mean that the Spirit asks one to do something one may not be prepared for. Take the case of the young carpenter, who decided that he really wanted to obey and follow the leadership of the Holy Spirit. Friday when he received his paycheck, the Holy Spirit was right there by his side with a unfamiliar request. "Don't take your pay check to the bank." The still small voice said to him, "Instead, take it to Dr. Graham, because he really needs your money today." The young carpenter who had decided that he would also like to walk by faith, and experience God's miracles in his life was speechless. Of course, the moment that still small voice made his request on the Father's behalf, guess who showed up, no other than the old devil himself. One thing one has to admit about the devil, he is always there, always on time to discredit God, and to tell one what a big fool one is going to make of one self. But the young carpenter said to himself, "I will go regardless, I will not give in to doubt or fear. When I give Dr. Graham my paycheck, I will tell him what I felt, and if I heard wrong, I feel sure he will tell me." When the young carpenter knocked on Dr. Graham's door, he was invited in. "Come in and sit down." Dr. Graham said, "I hope nothing is wrong?"

"Nothing at all," replied the young carpenter. "It's just that when I received my paycheck today, I thought that the Holy Spirit was saying to me, I should give it to you, I don't know why, and if I am wrong I sincerely apologize if I wasted your time."

Dr. Graham looked at him and said, "Son, you are not wasting my time, how much is your paycheck?" The young carpenter took it out of his pocket, and handed it to the doctor. Dr. Graham stretched his hand out taking the check and said, "Praise God, this is exactly the amount of money I have been asking God to give me. You see a week ago God asked me to give all the money I had available to someone else, and now He is meeting my need through you." Believe it or not, but it can be fun to totally depend on the Lord from day to day. Sometimes our lives are so scheduled and programmed, budgeted and managed, that we leave no room for God to intervene and maneuver. No wonder then that so often we have become the obstacle in the way of the Holy Spirit instead of being in the Master's service.

While we are begging and pleading for a miracle, praying and praying, while we bombard heaven with one cry after the other for help, only to find out that the heavens seems to be made out of brass. We feel like the prayers we pray falls on deaf ears. And we begin to wonder why God is not answering our prayers. In the book of Numbers 22-24, we read the story of a prophet who disobeyed God. When the angel of the Lord stood in the way of the donkey the prophet hit the donkey, until the donkey spoke to him and asked why he was being hit? All of a sudden Balaam also saw the Angel, who rebuked Balaam for his disobedience.

We must realize that if the Old Testament was written to us for a example, then we will see that God's intentions was always to bless his people, as God plainly declared to Israel in Deuteronomy 28. However, most of the time Israel rejected God's way. But Jesus came to tell us that now there is a opportunity for everyone to become partakers of the new covenant. Sadly, many Christians don't even realize what God has given them in the climactic battle in which Christ prevailed, to redeem you and me from the curse of the law. Jesus bought our freedom, we are no longer slaves to satanic unbelief, poverty, sickness, defeat and uncontrolled behavior. We no longer have to succumb to Satan's lies, or fear his retribution, because we are free! *Free at last, thank God I am free at last.* But like it is with everything else, with freedom comes new responsibilities, and obedience to the law.

Little Steps of Faith

> Jesus said, "Not every one that saith unto me Lord, Lord, shall enter into the kingdom of heaven; but he that doeth the will of my Father which is in heaven."
>
> Matthew 7:21

God is not asking for your sacrifice, rather He is asking to be your companion, and asking you to allow Him the opportunity to direct your life into success, and joy, by taking directions from your Creator, through the Holy Spirit, you allow God to help you to take *Little Steps Of Faith.*

> Lay not up for yourselves treasures upon the earth, where moth and rust doth corrupt, and where thieves break-through and steal: But lay up for yourselves treasures in heaven, where neither moth rust doth corrupt, and where thieves do not break through and steal: for where your treasure is, there will your heart be also.
>
> Matthew 6:19

> May be able to comprehend with all the saints what is the

breath and the length, and the depth and the height; And to know the love of Christ, which passeth knowledge, that ye might be filled with all the fullness of God. Now unto him that is able to do exceeding abundantly above all that we ask or think, according to the power that worketh in us, Unto him be glory in the church by Christ Jesus throughout ages, world without end.

Ephesians 3:18–21

To me the above scriptures contain some of the most beautiful words ever put on paper. To me it is saying that I am a child of the almighty God. My God is The One, Creator of heaven and earth. The God that is so organized that He and only He has a system in place that can count my hair. Think of it, every time I have a shower, or every time I brush my hair, God counts it and knows how many I have left. Try to imagine what it would take to devise a computerized contrivance with the ability to continuously keep accurate count of every hair of every human-being on the face of the earth. The most advanced technology to our disposal, or the greatest geniuses on the planet today, will find such a task impossible. Most likely they will declare such an idea ludicrous, outrageous, ridiculous, or an idea with no merit, and for good reason. If the God we serve is so meticulous, so interested in His children, and wants to be so intensely involved in our lives. If it is His expressed desire to do things for us, provide food for us, give us health, and technology, wisdom, success and happiness. When we can look all around us and see His creation in the sea, and on earth and in the stars and they all speak to us in one way or another. When with awe-some respect we observe the displays of God's extravaganza. His multiplicity of over abundance. His endless variety of extreme beauty. Why then does so few of His children even want to give Him the opportunity to bless them, or be willing to take Him up on His offer? *"Let this mind be in you, which was also in Christ Jesus"* (Philippians 2:5).

Try to comprehend the thoughts of Jesus, who never had to beg for an offering to support His gospel team. He never had to charge a seminar fee, or had to ask for a registration fee, or ask everyone to pay for their own meals at a banquet service. He asked His Father to multiply the loaves and fishes from a little boys lunch to feed the five thousand, (Luke 6:32). Jesus told Peter to catch a fish to pay their taxes (Matthew 17:27).

Will it be totally unreasonable to ask God to provide for us in similar ways, if we are about the Father's business as Jesus was? Remember, Jesus has already said to us, "Whatsoever you ask." *Whatsoever, is distinctly without qualification, or restriction.* Even though as a family we were getting by just fine, walking by faith would at times still get a little scary.

When one is a family of six as we were at the time, there is a never ending demand for all kinds of needs. We were living in our house that God had provided, but this Sunday we were down *to the very last of our food supplies.* Usually when I was not preaching, my family and I would go to the local church, where we regularly attended. That Sunday I had a call from someone I had met in a revival, who lived about four hours from where we lived. "Can we have lunch with you today?" The voice on the phone asked, "We have something we want to give you." The person continued. "If you're willing to share what we have, you are more than welcome" I replied, "And yes, we will be honored to have you and your family share our meal." I did not ask anybody for help, I did not mention my need to a living soul, only to a living God. I had no idea what the brother meant when he said that he had something he wanted to give us. After church when we pulled up in front of our home, our visitors were waiting.

After we all had lunch, which started out being barely enough for the six of us, but here we fed ten, and everyone had all they could eat, there was still plenty left over. The adults departed to the living room. They immediately started to share with us what God had put on their hearts to do. First the brother took a check out of his pocket, written for twenty-five hundred dollars to me for the ministry. Then he handed Genny a check for four hundred dollars.

At another occasion when we had no money to buy the children anything for Christmas, it was the day before Christmas when a check for two thousand dollars came in the mail.

One Wednesday evening when I had no place to preach, Genny and I went to a home Bible study. That day I had some bills that I needed to pay, and the only one who knew that I even needed money was God. I was never more surprised when the very evangelist from South Africa whom God had me to pay his family's airfare, two days before we were to leave for Bible College was also there. After the meeting he gave me six hundred dollars, he said the Lord told him to give it to me even before we arrived at the Bible study.

Many years ago before God called Genny and me into full-time ministry. The Lord told me to give four hundred dollars to my pastor. Now back in 1971, one could still buy a really decent car with four hundred dollars. I had promised Genny that I would buy her a car, and when I received a unexpected bonus of four hundred dollars from my employer, I thought I would buy Genny the car I had promised her. The one thing I had not count on was the Lord's interest in the four hundred dollars. Now the Lord only said to me once in that still small voice, which is so easy to ignore if one so chooses. The Lord said to me, "Give the four hundred dollars to your pastor" One thing about God, he is not going to beg one, or threaten one to comply. We already have

His word, and when we as His children refuse to comply, He will let us learn by our mistakes. Perhaps even let us wander off into the wilderness for a while like Israel did.

After that still small voice said to me, "Give the four hundred dollars to your pastor," I thought, "No this is not the Lord telling me to give four hundred dollars to my pastor, it's my imagination at work." Then I said, "Lord if this is you telling me to give my pastor the four hundred dollars, then speak louder, or knock me over the head, otherwise I am going to go ahead with my plans to buy Genny a car." Nothing happened, God did not even respond to my request. I went ahead and bought the car, paid the man in cash. Once I got the car home, I proudly showed Genny what I had bought for her. For some reason my father-in-law was also at the house that day. By trade he was a mechanical engineer, and loved to sail underneath anything with a engine and check it out. That was exactly what he did that day. He sailed under the car and started to tinker around. After just a few minutes he came sailing out from underneath the car and said to me, "Corrie, I don't know who you bought this piece of junk from, but if you want my advice, give it back before you put a another mile on it." I said, "Dad, what do you mean, the car runs really nice?" He said, "It makes no difference, because all four of the engine mountings are broken off, the engine can fall out any minute even as you are driving down the road."

If you ever did anything really stupid, like I just did, and you knew that it was the direct result of disobeying the Holy Spirit, then you will know how I felt. I had a hollow feeling on the pit of my stomach. I knew without a shadow of a doubt that I had failed God one more time. Without another word I drove the car back to the chap who I purchased the car from, and told him what was wrong with his car. The man who I purchased the car from without any quarrel or argument he returned my money to me. That day when I got back home, I said to my wife Genny, "Sweetheart, I am very sorry, but the Lord told me to give the four hundred dollars to the pastor in that "still small voice" and I did not want to do it. I was not really sure that it was God who was telling me to give the money to the pastor at the time. You know how badly I wanted to buy you a car of your own. But it seems the Lord had other plans. Will you go with me to the pastor's house, and we give this money to him?" Now this little diversion buying the car took about three days in all, listen to what the pastor said when I gave him the money. He said, "Thank you so much, you just don't know how we prayed for this four hundred dollars. It's three days late, but we can manage. God bless you." Before we left he wanted to pray with us, I almost felt to embarrassed to pray. I said, "Lord please forgive me."

On the other hand one appreciates it when whatever it was the Lord tells one to do gets confirmed. I must confess, if there is one thing I do not want to mess around with, it is with God's directions or His money. Sadly, all of God's children don't take that little still small voice very seriously. Consider this, if at any time you feel unsure if it is God telling you to do it, or perhaps you feel it's just you thinking it. Consider the fact that it is impossible to out give God, for He promised a hundred fold return. Since that particular experience, I decided to rather give too much than too little. Why? Because with obedience comes God's blessings.

This also reminds me of another incident, where the shoe as to speak was on the other foot. Let me tell you what happened to me one time when I prayed for money and did not get it. A banker once told me that the people with the worst credit ratings are preachers and police officers. Of course, the banker might also understand why, if he knew anything about walking by faith. I had a car on which I had a bank loan and I really did not want to get behind on my monthly payments. It came up to the very day my car payment was due, it was the very last day, and the money for the payment just did not come in. I said Lord, "Where is my car payment?" The Lord said, "Wait and I will show you." That same day I was visited by three different brothers, independently during the course of the day each one of the three who came to visit with me said that the Lord had told them to give me some money. Each one also told me the amount the Lord had told them to give to me. After I totaled the amounts each of the three brothers was to give me, I would have had my car payment. But each of them had some excuse. They said, "The Lord told me to give you x amount of dollars, but each one said, before they got around to give me the money, they had spent it, the one said his wife had spent it. Now remember, I did not approach them, they freely volunteered their confessions. But that was the way God used, to let me understand, that it was not His fault. The fault was with His beloved children, for whom He prepared eternity. Why were they disobedient? Good question and a problem many of God's children struggle with. I don't believe they did it on purpose, rather, I think it is a question of uncertainty or procrastination. Not obeying God's direction should be considered a diversion from the enemy, and could cost the believer dearly in other ways unforeseen at that time. To prevent the enemy from coming in and finding something to steal from me and diverting money earmarked for the work of the Lord, I now try to do what God tells me to do without first thinking about it. After all when I sow, I will also reap. Now it just makes sense that if I sow bountifully, I will also reap bountifully.

Jesus said in Matthew 7:21:

"Not every one that saith unto me, Lord, Lord, shall enter

into the kingdom of heaven; but he that doeth the will of my Father which are in heaven."

Paul tells us in Romans 15:18, 19:

"For I will not dare to speak of any of those things which Christ has not wrought by me, to make the Gentiles obedient, by word and deed. Through mighty signs and wonders, by the power of the Spirit of God."

Think of it this way. Obedience always presents a challenge, once I as God's child have met that challenge, I then have also given God the opportunity to bless me with a miracle. Miracles produces testimonies, which on the other hand diminish Satan's chances to derail you. Miracles and testimonies also create a witness tool that will win new souls into God's kingdom.

Is it any wonder that the church of Jesus Christ has so little life? Why do we have churches full of sick people, and broke people and spiritually hungry people? Why don't we see more miracles, signs and wonders? Are we paying the price for disobedience or are we insensitive to the nudging of the Holy Spirit? Perhaps many in the church are already caught-up in the spirit of Laodicea. Just lukewarm, neither hot nor cold. "Behold I stand at the door and knock; if any man hear my voice, and open the door, I will come into him, and will sup with him, and he with me" (Revelation 3:20).

Ask yourself, "Am I sensitive to that still small voice? Do I act on that still small voice in obedience, or disobey out of fear?" Perhaps you say, "I never hear that still small voice." If that is the case, you might just have to take some time with the Lord and wait on Him until you can hear His voice for yourself.

Six Nuns and a Priest

> But the Comforter, which is the Holy Ghost, whom the Father will send in my name, he shall teach you all things, and bring all things to your remembrance, whatsoever I have said unto you.
>
> John 14:26

During 1979 the Lord dramatically changed our ministry. The Lord told me that if I believed that He multiplied the loaves and the fishes. And if I believe that he turned water into wine. And if I believed, "That whatsoever ye shall ask in my name, that I will do, that the Father may be glorified in the Son" (John 14:13).

That if I believe those things, I could have a seminar, and not charge a dime. I could provide all the food and accommodations in any hotel of my choice without charging the participants a single penny. "Don't charge them one penny." The Lord told me. "Only take one offering after the seminar is over. Give everyone an opportunity to give at the end of the seminar, but only the ones who want to give. Tell everyone who comes that you will have a special meeting only for those who feel in their hearts that God wants them to give towards the seminar."

I get very scared when God tells me to do unconventional

things. I would much rather do things that I know about. I also found out that when the Lord gives one something to do that is unconventional, that it is also better to keep the instructions God gives one to one self. I told one of my closest friends what the Lord told me to do, and he thought I was taking faith too far.

Within a few days I had made arrangements with the Quality Inn, a brand new hotel that was just completed. I booked a block of fifty rooms, reserved the conference room, and selected the menus. The manager figured the cost for +/- fifty couples at over eight thousand dollars. Not a lot of money to some big ministries. But when one is a small fry like me, eight thousand dollars is a lot of money. I was hoping that the hotel would not require a deposit, because I did not have a deposit to put down. After all the arrangements was made I left, thankful no one mentioned a down payment. But the next day the manager called me and said, "I forgot to ask you for a down payment, but never mind," He said, "I trust you." "Just as well," I thought to myself. I mailed five thousand invitations out during the next week. I told my guests that all the expenses for this seminar was on me. If they could get to the airport in Tulsa where the seminar was to take place. I also told them in my letter, that I will provide the transportation from the airport to the hotel. I provide the rooms and all the food, no charge. My one friend who I shared my mission with said, "All you will get will be a bunch of people who are looking for a free vacation, and you will be stuck with the bill."

Four weeks later we had about one hundred and ten people to share the block of fifty rooms. Our seminar started on a Thursday evening, through Sunday morning. Every one who came stayed for the entire time, and attended all the services. Even though I encouraged people not to come to the Sunday morning offering unless the Lord specifically instructed them to participate, they all came. The most amazing thing I experienced was the day of the offering. Every one already knew what they were going to give. They said that God had told them what to give. A few of the people who had nothing to give were given money by others in the group, so they could also participate in the giving. A few people placed their jewelry in the offering. The fears of my friend proved unwarranted. After everyone was gone and we counted the offering, we had sufficient money to meet our obligations. A miracle? Yes, I would say so. But also a God who stands by His word. Absolutely! By His word and you can trust Him, without a doubt.

Several other miracles also took place. I could hardly believe my ears when a Catholic Priest and six Nuns arrived from the airport. Since the seminar was advertised as a marriage seminar, primarily for couples, the last person one would expect to see would be a nun or a Priest. But when God starts to work, sense doesn't always make sense anymore. The Holy Spirit will find a way to minister to everyone's individual needs, no matter how it may differ from whatever the subject of teaching may be. That Saturday morning during the seminar, I was approached by the Catholic Priest and the six Nuns. "Will you baptize us?" They wanted to know. Caught totally by surprise, I said, "Baptize you! what made you decide that you should get baptized?" "Well," they said, "we have been doing some serious scripture research and praying here for the past several days, and we feel that this is what God wants us to do. Another thing, when we go back to our Monastery, we won't have anyone who will baptize us." I said, "The only place here is the hotel swimming pool, and for that we should get permission from the manager." They had no problem with that, even though they were upper middle age, they all strutted down to the managers office like a few very excited children to obtain permission to be baptized in the motel swimming pool.

That evening the manager circulated a notice to all hotel guests that the swimming pool will be of limits between 8 a.m. and 9 a.m. for a baptismal service. The next morning when we assembled at the swimming pool for the baptism, scores of people were standing on the balconies to observe the event. "Can any man forbid water, that these should be baptized in the name of the Lord" (Acts 10:47).

During another seminar, the Lord manifested His presence in a way I have never seen before or since. We also had a group of about one hundred, everyone was happy and praising the Lord. The singing time was over and I thought that it was time for me to start the teaching. I stepped up to the microphone and waved my hand, and I was going to say, "You may sit down." But before I could get a word out of my mouth, a rush of what felt like air, it made a slight sucking noise, at that same instant I saw people all over falling down. Except about five or six people were still standing, all the rest were on the floor. The five or six who were still standing looked just as surprised as I was. Realizing something supernatural was taking place they also fell to their knees and started to pray. People were lying in between the seats, in the isle, some were lying half on top of one another. I just stood there in amazement. Nothing like this has ever happened to me before or since. About fifteen to twenty minutes later people started to get back up. Happy! Everyone was happy all of a sudden. I was still just standing there, like I was dumb struck. Then people started to jump up and tell what happened to them. A man blind since birth said he could see, another man who was deaf said he could hear, some were set free from depression and experienced a joy they never had before, and on and on everyone had something they wanted to praise the Lord for. "And they went forth, and preached every where, and the Lord working with them, and confirming the word with signs following" (Mark 16:20).

His Grace Is Sufficient For Me

The apostle Paul speaking about his affliction and his inability to overcome writes, "For this thing I besought the Lord thrice, that it might depart from me. And He said unto me, My grace is sufficient for thee: for my strength is made perfect in weakness" (2 Corinthians 12:8, 9).

The most important thing for any child of God is to learn to trust Him and to realize that He is always with me. Immaterial to how I feel at the time. Some times I don't feel His presence and I wonder where He is. At times I pray and I feel no contact, no connection and I wonder why? At times I wonder why it is that I can not feel connected. My prayers feel like empty bubbles floating off into nowhere and disintegrate prematurely. But then again, I am reminded that it is by faith. My walk with God is by faith. The apostle Paul also tells us that: "Through faith we understand that the worlds were framed by the word of God, so that things which are seen were not made of things which do appear" (Hebrews 11:3).

In the New Testament in contemporary language by Eugene H. Peterson, the same scripture reads like this "By faith, we see the world called into existence by God's word, what we see is created by what we don't see." Allow me to give you one more translation, the Amplified Version.

How does this thing called faith then really work? Have you

ever thought that; If only I had faith? Well, have you? Well, you don't need to want it, or wish for it. God already gave it to you. We all start out with the same amount of faith according to the word of God.

In Acts 10:34 we read, "Then Peter opened his mouth, and said, Of a truth I perceive that God is no respecter of persons." In God's eyes you and me and every person is equal. It is impossible for God to like you any better than he likes me, or treat you with more concessions than he would allow me.

The Apostle Paul says in Romans 12:3:

> For I say through the grace given unto me, to every man that is among you, not to think of himself more highly than he ought to think, but to think soberly, according as God hath dealt to every man the measure of faith.

Equality is the word. I am as equal as you are, you are as equal as any person of faith who ever lived. So! where is the difference? I believe in the application or willingness to venture out into the unknown. Venture into the unfamiliar. Allow the invisible hand of God to guide one into the unseen. This entire issue of faith depends exclusively on, how far am I willing to trust God?

What then makes one person exercise God's word above that of another person. One time I was out of a job, many years ago when my oldest child was still in her first grade. I left the house with these words to Genny, "I don't know how long I will be gone, but when you see me next time I will have a job." We lived in a small town in the Cape Province of South Africa. Genny took me to the train station where I bought a ticket to Cape Town. I had no idea where to find a job. After several hours on the train I found a news paper someone left behind. Paging through the job section I saw a hospital in Johannesburg advertising for a Director for their food service division. I said to myself "This is my job." Once I arrived in Cape Town, I immediately bought myself a ticket to Johannesburg, which was one thousand miles from Cape Town where I was at the present time. I arrived in Johannesburg the very last day on which they accepted applications. The paper said to write and mail a resume, but since I had no time to do that, I just had to go in person. I got myself a cab at the Johannesburg train station, and arrived at the hospital about thirty minutes later. When I told the secretary in the office my predicament, and the fact that I came a thousand miles to get my application in on time, she immediately arranged for me to see the administrator. As I walked into this man's office who I could swear I did not know from a bar of soap. I could not believe my ears when the man said to me, "I thought your name sounded familiar. We were together at a military camp." For a while we talked about the good old days, but still I could not place the man. However, I was too embarrassed to say so, specially since he was so glad to see me. When I told him how I found out about the job, he was equally impressed and said, "Don't say another word, the job is yours." Some may say luck, but I want to say this, when you have made up your mind and launch out in faith, God is going to be there for you.

Angels or Men?

> Likewise the Spirit also helpeth our infirmities, for we know not what we should pray for as we ought, but the Spirit itself maketh intercession for us.
>
> Romans 8:26

It was during the latter part of the seventies when the Lord spoke to me one day and said, "I want you to conduct a city wide crusade in Grand Island, Nebraska." I said, "Lord, how will I do that? I have only been to one crusade in all of my life and that was when I was just a young boy. I had no idea what to do. In fact I would not even know how to get started." The Lord answered me and said, "I will send you to Morris Curello, there you will learn how to do a crusade." I thought about it for a moment and asked again, "Lord, who is Morris Curello, and where will I find him?" The Lord replied, "Wait and I will send a messenger to show you."

That was the end of the conversation between the Lord and myself. The whole experience left me with butterflies in my stomach. I had the feeling that something very strange was about to take place. I did not want to tell anyone what had happened out of fear that no one would believe me. So I decided to keep the information to myself. However, I was very curious to find out if anyone at least knew this Morris Curello who ever he was. I few days later I asked some church folks if they had ever heard of a Morris Curello. They said they did, but could not say where his offices were. They said they knew that he was a big time Evangelist, but that he has never been in the Oklahoma's to their knowledge. Some what satisfied that I at least found out that there was such a person, I decided to just wait until I hear from the Lord again.

Three months must have past. When one day I had been out on a few errands, on returning, I stopped in the drive way of my house and saw my wife Genny on the front porch. She waved at me to open the car window, as I did she shouted, "You had a phone call while you were out. There is a chap at the Grey Hound bus station who wants you to come and get him, his name is Frank. He said Pastor Frank, he is visiting the States from India."

I backed my car into the street to go and meet the stranger who called me, wondering who he was. After arriving at the Grey Hound bus terminal, it did not take me long to locate him, I already knew that he was a Indian man from India. There was only a few people at the bus station when I got there. I targeted a man who looked like an Indian to me, and walked up to him and asked, "Are you Pastor Frank?" The man readily replied, "Yes and you must be Pastor Corrie?" After greeting each other, I started to escort Pastor Frank to where my car was parked, but noticed that he only had a brief case and a Bible. So I asked him, "Can I help you to get the rest of your luggage?" To which he replied, "This is all my luggage, I travel light as the Lord has instructed me to." He then quoted me this scripture, "Provide neither gold nor silver, nor brass in your purses, nor script for your journey, neither two coats, neither shoes, nor yet stave's: for the workman is worthy of his meat" (Matthew 10:9, 10).

On the way home Br. Frank told me a little bit about his work in India where he pastors a small church in a rural community. I wanted to know why he called me to meet him at the Greyhound bus terminal and how he knew where to find me. He told me how two complete strangers walked up to him at the airport in New York City, and asked him where he was going. After he told them where he was going, they said to him that they had a good friend who is living in Tulsa, Oklahoma, and gave him a piece of paper with my name and phone number. They then asked him to promise that he would stop over in Tulsa and meet me. Quite surprised I asked him, "Who were these two men who asked you to come and see me in Tulsa?" To which he replied, "I have no idea." I said, "Br. Frank to my knowledge I don't know anybody who lives in New York City, how did it happened that these men came up to you any way?" Br. Frank looked at me a little sheepishly and said, "Pastor Corrie, I did not have time to ask them any questions, after they handed me the piece of paper, I looked at it just for a second, and when I looked up to ask them who they were, they were gone. How they could have disappeared so quick, I don't know." I was taken back somewhat and wondered if Br. Frank made up the story or if it was really true. However, I did not say anything more to him about it.

Sometimes one meets all kinds of weird people in the ministry. Br. Frank not having any luggage and calling me with such a strange story seemed to fit the profile. However, the next morning after breakfast, Br. Frank said, "Pastor Corrie, around ten o'clock will you please take me back to the bus station?" I said, "Sure Br. Frank, but what is the rush, stay for a few more days." "Well," Br. Frank said, "I can't, tomorrow is the first day of the ministers workshop in Dallas to be given by Morris Curello. I have come all the way from India just for that, and that is why I have to leave today." I could feel the hair on the back of my neck standing straight up. Shivers ran up my spine as if someone had threw a bucket of ice cold water on me, I could not have been more surprised. I wanted to say something, but the words were sticking in my dry mouth. My mind was racing at the speed of lightning. Was this the way the Lord was telling me where to find Morris Curello. I have been waiting patiently for months, praying and asking God to show me where to find this Evangelist. Now this funny looking man from India with one squint eye. Was this the messenger of God who He said He was going to send to tell me where I can find Morris Curello?! And the two men at the airport, who could they have been, Angels? This was too strange for words. Finally I was able to break a sound out of my dry throat and said, "Br. Frank, that is where I am supposed to go to. Can I still go or is it too late?" "No, Pastor Corrie." Frank said, "It is not too late, Morris Curello is a good friend of mine and I can bring anyone I choose to the workshop. If you want to go just tell me and when I get there I will have your name placed into the register and because you are my friend the seminar will be free, no charge to you. If you want the directions I have it here."

After I dropped Br. Frank off at the bus station I thought to myself, "God can make things look so simple at times." Why God would choose such a strange way to direct me was beyond anything that made any sense to me. But God is my Father and He knows more than I do. My next question was what was He teaching me and was I learning through this?

God was teaching me that I was not on a one man mission, there are other members of the body, His body, that must participate. Scripture teach us that Christ is the head of this body. Paul says, "For as the body is one, and hath many members, and all the members are of one body, being many are one body, so also is Christ" (1 Corinthians 12:12).

Dakes Annotated Reference notes states, "You and all in Christ like you make the true church or the body of Christ." When the Holy Spirit is in control in a Church, He, the Holy Spirit will also keep the church moving forward. The reason I believe we have so many *dead* churches is due to Pastors who want to be in control. Always afraid that without them at the helm, the ship will sink. Too often in today's church there is the spirit of Jezebel in control, rejecting the true prophets of God and thereby preventing the body of Christ to grow up. I have experienced that, once we learn that every one of us in the church, including Pastors and Evangelists, understand that He, Jesus gave the Holy Spirit to us for the purpose of leading and teaching. His control might not always fit our own theology, but He will accomplish far more than we ever could without Him. Let the five fold ministry operate freely. God knows exactly what He is doing, and will not allow the church services to turn into a circus.

An Offering without Equal

Now that I knew where Morris Curello was holding his ministerial conference, and I had the invitation given to me by Br. Frank, I only had one more problem. I was without money. God's direction could not have come at a worse time for me. I calculated my cost to go and even though I had friends at Christ for the Nations in Dallas Texas who said that they would accommodate me, I needed at least fifty more dollars. I prayed and told the Lord that I have been waiting all these months to get the directions to go to Morris Curello, and now that I have the directions I don't have the money to go.

I learned later that even while I was praying, God was already discussing my need to another member of the body of Jesus Christ. I no sooner got off of my knees when someone rang the doorbell. I opened the door and there was Dick, a member of the Disciples of Christ church I was pastoring. I invited Dick inside, without greeting he started to complain and said to me, "What is so urgent that I have to give my only fifty dollars to you?" I said, "Why Dick what do you mean?" Dick said, "I was selling a camper I had for fifty dollars, after the man looked at it he went to his house to get the money and while he was gone the Lord said to me, Dick! Corrie needs the money more than you do, go and give it to him." Dick continued to tell me how inconvenient it was and he said, "I told the Lord that I also needed the money, but if Corrie needed it more than I do, I will give it to him on one condition. The man pays me in a one fifty-dollar note. If he brings the money in any other combination I keep it. Well, the man came back with a fifty-dollar note. At least can you tell me what you need it for?" Dick asked. I said, "Certainly: Dick, some months ago the Lord told me to go to Morris Curello, I just found out today that he is having a ministerial conference starting tomorrow and I have to be there." After knowing the details, Dick left, happy that he could be a part of whatever it was God was doing, even if it meant parting with his money.

At the ministerial conference I was mainly listening for the details I needed to have to setup and conduct a city wide crusade. Since that was not one of the topics listed on the program that was offered, I had to take what I could get, in whatever order it came to me. By the end of the conference I had several pages full of details Morris Curello shared and felt sure that I received what I came for. But like every good Evangelist, before the conference was dismissed, Morris Curello took up an offering. He did not take any offerings during the conference and told everyone that he wanted only those present that were truly interested in helping his ministry to participate in giving. I was not particularly planning on giving anything, since I barely had enough money to get back home.

Genny and I sat there and waited for the meeting to finish when the Lord said to me, "You should also give, for when you do your crusade you would expect others to give." I looked in my pockets to see what I had, I had to get home and needed to keep money for gas. However, that was when I heard Morris Curello say, "If you are here to give, I expect you to make your giving worthwhile, I don't need any small change. Listen to me, I want you to give at least three hundred dollars or don't give at all. If you don't have three hundred dollars or more on you, then you can go to the back and fill out a pledge with one of the counselors. But before you give, I want to pray with you, I also want you to understand that this is serious business. This is what I will do. I will ask God to bless you according to Deuteronomy 28. However, if you fill out a pledge and then you don't send me my money, I will also ask God to let the curse come on you according to Deuteronomy 28." I had never heard a minister talk like that before in my life. I looked at Genny and she looked at me. I said to her, "What do you think I should do, the Lord told me to give, but three hundred dollars is too much." She just shrugged her shoulders and said, "That's up to you." Feeling that I had no other option but to obey the Lord, I went to where the counselors were and pledged my three hundred dollars.

About eight that evening after several hours on the road driving home we pulled up in the driveway of our home in Tulsa. We had no sooner stepped through the front door when the phone rang, I picked it up and it was Dick on the other end. He said, "Corrie, can I please come and see you?" I replied "Dick, we just walked in the door and we are really tired, can it wait until tomorrow?" "No" Dick said, "It just cannot wait. Lilly and I have been trying to get you all afternoon, I must see you now, I promise we won't be long." I said, "O.K. if you promise because I am tired." Fifteen minutes later I heard a car door slam, seconds later the door bell rang and I went to the door to let them in. After the greetings Dick said, "We were just getting ready to write the rent check for our landlord when the Lord said to both Lilly and I, "Give that money to Corrie, he needs it more than you do, I will supply money for your rent in another way." So that is why we had to see you tonight" They both sat there looking at me for a sign of approval. I said, "How much money do you have to give me?" Almost simultaneously they replied, "Three hundred dollars." I almost fell out of my chair, this thing was getting more complicated by the minute. I began to wonder just how important that Grand Island crusade was to God, and why He would choose someone like me who has never done a crusade before. However, I knew that I had to obey the Holy Spirit, even if I did not fully understand the reason. God's word tells us that obedience produces righteousness,

> "Know ye not, that to whom ye yield yourselves servants ye are to whom ye obey; whether of sin unto death, or of obedience unto righteousness?"
>
> Romans 6:16

The ultimate challenge to the believer is in these words of Jesus,

> "But lay up for yourselves treasures in heaven, where neither moth nor rust doth corrupt, and where thieves do not break through and steal: For where your treasure is there will your heart be also."
>
> Matthew 6:20

Dick and Lily had certainly opened themselves to receive multiple blessings, exceedingly abundantly above all they asked or think. I told Dick and Lilly that I had pledged three hundred dollars as I was directed by that still small voice. They said they understood and was glad that God even thought them worthy to participate in a multiple body ministry as this. Anticipating a heavenly blessing from God for obedience, I said to Dick and

Lilly, that it would be only fair for us to pray and ask God to share the blessing that will follow with them.

I had all the direction and confirmation I possibly needed to take the next step to start to put together the Grand Island crusade. I felt a great excitement of being in the place where God wanted me to be for that moment in time. I can not describe it, but it is a feeling of joy and confidence that you know for yourself that you had been with God. You know in your spirit man that something really great is about to take place and nothing but nothing that the circumstances around dictates makes any difference whatsoever. I still had no money and I reminded the Lord that it will take a lot of money to put the crusade together. But I also praised the Lord that I knew what His word says, and I was confident that my God shall supply all the money that I needed to put this crusade together.

Even though I had no money I had this feeling of confidence and overwhelming joy inside me. It was that kind of feeling that I was at this time in my life chosen by God for a special purpose. I felt that everything was going to fall in place. All I had to do was to trust the Lord and follow the direction of my *Senior Partner. {The Holy Spirit}*

The following week I received the two hundred dollars my church paid me weekly as their Pastor. I gave Genny a hundred dollars for food and I kept a hundred. Early Monday morning I was in my car and on my way to Grand Island Nebraska. I had never been to that state before and wondered what I would find? I had until Saturday to work on putting together a crusade, Sunday I had to be back at church to preach. I drove straight through to Grand Island and found a cheap motel room for fifteen dollars per night. The following morning bright and early I scouted out the land, the town was small and had nothing for rent that I could find that would be suitable for a crusade. That same day I arranged with one of the restaurants to set up a breakfast meeting and invited about twenty pastors from different churches to attend. I was using the direction I received from the ministerial workshop. To my surprise all the Pastors I invited to the breakfast came.

At the breakfast I briefly told them that I was in the process of setting up a crusade and invited the Pastors who could assist me to stay behind, the others could leave. One of the Pastors asked, "How many of these crusades have you conducted in the past." I had to admit that I was attempting to do it for the first time. Every one thanked me for breakfast and got up and left except one Pastor. I realized my enthusiasm as God's ambassador, a secret agent under cover in God's secret kingdom, went over like a lead balloon and that I was going to do the crusade by myself. Except, that was for Pastor Arny. He pulled up a chair next to mine and said to me, "Don't worry, this bunch would not help Jesus if He appeared in person." Then he began to tell me that Grand Island was a very hard place. He said several ministries came through Grand Island over the past several years for the purpose to conduct a city wide crusade and not one had any attendance. He also told me that two of the ministries left their bills unpaid. Pastor Arny gave me a little advice and said, "Only you know if God really told you to do this. If you are sure that God indeed told you to have this crusade then I will support you with my prayers and help you with the music end during the crusade. If God did not tell you to put this crusade together, I suggest you don't try it, we had enough of a bad taste by what has been tried here in the past."

I thanked Pastor Arny and he and I said a short prayer for me before taking his leave from me. As I was leaving to get to my car, I said to the Lord, "Well Lord, what now, no one is going to help me?" I drove back to the downtown area not knowing what to do. That was when I spotted a small movie Theater. I pulled my car into a parking space to see if I could ask someone inside if the Theater was for rent. Inside I met Dexter, a big husky fellow who was cleaning the Theater. Dexter looked more like he should be on a football field than cleaning the movie Theater. Dexter was very friendly, after greeting him I told him I was there to inquire if the Theater could be rented. Dexter looked at me and said, "They won't rent you this Theater, but tell me what do you need it for?" I started to tell him about my intentions to put together a crusade. Before I could say more he held up his hand and stopped me: Dexter said, "Lets go next door and get a cup of coffee, I am due for a break."

After we got seated in a little dingy coffee shop that smelt more like cow pasture than a coffee shop, I started again to tell Dexter why I was there. I could not help noticing the excitement building in Dexter as I was talking. Dexter did not want to know how many crusades I had conducted in the past. As soon as I finished, Dexter enthusiastically endorsed the crusade and pledged his overwhelming support. "I know where you can have your crusade." Dexter said, "Come with me and I will show you." We drove a few miles out of town and stopped in front of a race track. "This is the only place in town that is available." Dexter pointed to a large indoor area. Nothing was locked up and we walked inside and found ourselves in a large room big enough to hold a thousand people. "We can get this place." Dexter said, "And they may even let me have it for no charge if we promise to clean it up when we done." It looked good enough to me and I told Dexter that the racetrack was exactly what I was looking for.

After seeing the hall at the racetrack we went back to the coffee shop to discuss the rest of the details. Then I discovered that Dexter also worked for the local newspaper, just a "coincidence" ha! ha! Dexter was the man in charge of the newspaper companies advertising department. The paper only came out once a week and I told Dexter, what I wanted was a full page advertisement running for four weeks. I gave him the layout for the advertisement I had already prepared and he promised he would take care of it. Next I told Dexter that I would like to get a few billboards strategically located to cover every entrance and exit to the town. Dexter said he needed to make a phone call, to the man who owned the billboards. Several minutes later he came back and said that he can get eight billboards and that he thought that would be sufficient coverage. I agreed and asked him what all that would cost? I knew that I had no money, and even now, it will still take a miracle from heaven to place all the advertisement on nothing more than a friendly handshake. But at the same time I also realized that my God was a miracle working God who would take care of everything. Mine was not blind faith just to test God's word. What I was doing was pre-directed by the Holy Spirit. I had been assigned a secret mission to destroy enemy territory. My commanding officer and Senior partner would make sure that this entire operation will go off as planned. No one can prevent a successful completion, except me, and only if I miss His direction. But I plan to follow His direction carefully, and spoil Satan's stronghold. In the spoils there will hopefully be souls saved and rescued from the portholes of Hell. Dexter was God's point man. When none of the Pastors volunteered their participation except pastor Arny, God took over and gave me Dexter, a young Lutheran who told me that he had just recently received the infilling of the Holy Spirit. To me it was very obvious that Dexter's lamp was burning brightly. Dexter was waiting and ready for any chance to serve his Lord. After Dexter had time to figure up the cost, he said the total cost would be no more than two thousand dollars and I need not worry about it. He said my credit was good as far as he was concerned and I would receive a bill after the crusade. Wow! I could hardly believe my ears.

The scripture rang loud and clear for me, "All things are really possible to them that believe." Yet I knew that I could not possibly have done any of the things that happened that morning if God did not take charge. The Holy Spirit who is my Senior partner directed me successfully. Mission accomplished.

My joy knew no bounds. I went back to my motel room, gathered my luggage and departed for home. It was only Wednesday, when I left Monday I thought that it might take more than one trip to set up the crusade and here three days later everything was taken care of. That was providing Dexter does what he said he would do. "Well," I thought to myself, "I am positive that God gave Dexter to me to help me and that God would make sure everything gets done accordingly."

What a mighty God we serve! I was singing and praising the Lord as I drove mile after mile going home. At times I was so happy, tears of joy would well up in my eyes, my heart was leaping for joy. I knew that if I was realistic I would worry about this whole thing. I did not know Dexter and I had no way to know if the crusade would be successful and no way to get hold of two thousand dollars if it failed. But non of those thoughts once came to me. Jesus said, "If ye have faith as a grain of mustard seed" (Matthew 17:20).

Have you ever felt special, or chosen? That was how I felt. God was having me do things I never thought possible. The Holy Spirit reminded me that all of God's children were chosen. Jesus said, "Ye have not chosen me but I have chosen you, and ordained you that you should go and bring forth fruit, and that your fruit should remain: that whatsoever ye ask of the Father in my name, He may give it to you" (John 15:16).

The Day of the Big Crusade

It was Tuesday morning, one month later. Dexter assured me on the phone that all the arrangements were in place. He said people were talking about the crusade all around town. Dexter also told everyone that he knew the South African who was coming and that he, Dexter, had a big part in putting the crusade together. For the first time since that day my stomach was feeling queasy. I had never held a crusade before. But that was not my greatest concern. My greatest concern was that this is the day of the crusade, and I did not have enough money to fill the two engine Cessna plane with gas. A friend of mine had offered to fly me with all my crusade materials in his private plane. All I had to do was to put sixty dollars worth of gas in the plane. Today was that day and I did not have sixty dollars. I knew God knew I did not have sixty dollars. After all Jesus already told us, "For your heavenly Father knoweth that ye shall have need of all these things" (Matthew 6:32).

I said a short prayer to remind my Father that I knew that he would give me the money for the gas, "Jesus, you said," "If ye shall ask any thing in my name, I will do it." I am asking you for the sixty dollars to fill the plane with gas, amen."

After I had all my crusade materials together, I left for the airport. It was about 7 am. and I had about a thirty-minute drive to the airport. By the time I got to the runway, the brother who was flying me with his plane was already there checking on the plane. I greeted him and wondered if I should tell him that I did not have the sixty dollars to fill up the plane with gas. But somehow I could not bring myself around to say that. Instead, I immediately started to load the crusade materials from my car into the plane. After the plane was loaded he informed me that he was going to taxi the plane to the gas pumps and directed me, pointing with his finger where the office was where I had to pay for the gas. Again I thought that I should tell him that I had no money.

Still agonizing over what I should do, I watched the pilot as he pulled off with the plane down the runway. I was standing there feeling totally helpless, I prayed again and said, "Lord it is time for me to pay for the gas, what do you want me to do?" I looked up after my short prayer and I saw a car coming speeding down the runway towards me. It did not take me long to recognize the car as Dick's. The car came to a screeching halt. Dick rolled down his window. "I am glad I still found you." He said,

"I was afraid that I might miss you, the Lord told me to give you this sixty dollars. Is this the amount you need?" I said, "Yes! this is exactly what I need to fill the tank of the plane with gas for the trip to Grand Island."

I thanked Dick for being the one to rescue me for the umpteenth time and wondered why God was only using Dick every time? Dick left and I walked to the office where I had to pay for the gas. The pilot never knew that I had no money, neither did anyone else know that the entire crusade had been put together without one penny of my money.

As we took off in the Cessna, my heart was leaping with joy, my mouth was filled with praise. But I wondered why God always had to wait until the last second of the last minute. Waiting until the last possible moment was not the kind of excitement that I was looking for. But as it may, I felt that the Lord was very close to me. I had this overwhelming expectancy that I was tossed into unknown territory. Special Agent on assignment. I sensed the wings of Angels under the Cessna, and that deep down feeling that the everlasting arms of someone much bigger than I was in control here. This crusade was going to invade enemy territory. Demons by now were on full alert and working feverishly to come up with a counter action. However, the Lord and I had already taken the necessary steps to invoke the power of His word, commanding all demon activity to cease.

I had commanded Satan in the name of Jesus not to interfere in people's financial affairs, and not to hinder them in any way if they wanted to come to the crusade. "And the seventy returned again with joy, saying, Lord, even the devils are subject unto us through thy name" (Luke 10:17).

Even the great 007, "James Bond the best spy story Hollywood could cook up, possessed absolutely no comparison to this mission. I felt chosen, specially chosen by God to go into territory long held by God's enemy, to expose the evil works of the Devil and all his demons. That thought alone made me very happy. I knew that Satan himself still has not forgotten how he had been tormented by the Son of God. When he realized too late that the One he had killed on the cross was the Son of God and that Jesus had risen from the dead. Through the centuries, God always had a army of believers who were not afraid to use their authority and the name of Jesus. Relentlessly continuing the assault on Satan to take back the Children of God held as captives by the enemy. Here in the making was one more assault coming up! One more victory for the army of God!

I myself had not forgotten how Satan tormented me and my family in the past and that was another reason why I knew that it was going to give me immeasurable pleasure, every time, even one soul gets saved during this crusade. This time it was my turn to hurt Satan back and drive him out and divide the spoils amongst the bretheren.

> If ye abide in me, and my words abide in you, ye shall ask what ye will, and it shall be done unto you.
>
> John 15:7
>
> These things have I spoken unto you, that my joy might remain in you, and that your joy might be full.
>
> John 15:11
>
> Ye have not chosen me, but I have chosen you, and ordained you that you should go and bring forth fruit, and that your fruit should remain: that whatsoever ye shall ask of the Father in my name, He may give it you.
>
> John 15:16

The greatest story ever told. The greatest partnership ever formed. The easiest underlying guidelines [laws and bylaws]--- [policies and procedures]. "The New Covenant partnership to include you and me, an idea that was conceived by the Father. Purchased and sealed by the blood of Jesus Christ. Activated by the Holy Ghost, and ratified by God's only Son. Sealed for eternity in Holy blood, it remains in effect still today. Few demands are made from the junior stockholders. The greatest benefits of this covenant favors the junior partners [you and me] with equal opportunity for every participant. Equal shares to all who accept. Your and my only investment in this covenant is our tattered life of sin. Our dividends will be rewarded with glory throughout eternity, time without end.

Official backup on earth by celestial Angels on assignment is an added benefit, they are always near when needed. They are coming to us as Celestial soldiers from the greatest army in the universe, which consists of legions of Angels in fiery chariots to guarantee your and my successes against any army of demons for whatever onslaught they attempt.

> And when the servant of the man of God was risen early, and gone forth, behold a host compassed the city both with horses and with chariots. And his servant said unto him, Alas my master! how shall we do. And he said, fear not: for they that be with us are more than they that be with them. And Elisha prayed, and said Lord, I pray thee, open the eyes of the young man; and he saw: and, behold, the mountain was full of horses and chariots of fire around about Elisha.
>
> 2 Kings 6:15–17

Get your secret weapons, James Bond. Get your space wars United States. Get your demon hoards Devil! None of you, no not even one of you have the slightest chance of winning against God's celestial armies. Lets face the facts. World powers have tried to stop God's army, the governments of the world have tried to stop God's armies. Through the centuries there were those who tried to stop the army of God. The anti-Christ movement abolished prayer and the Bible in our U.S. schools, they refuse to teach our children about God's creation. But God's army is still moving on. Through the centuries the soldiers of the cross have been burned on stakes, nailed to crosses, fed to lions, but that army is still marching forward. Some of God's soldiers had gone to the most remote areas on earth to recruit soldiers, in their attempts they lost their lives, some were eaten by cannibals, some were overcome by sickness, but still the army of God remains unstoppable. Every attempt by Satan to stop this army has failed, and God's army is still pushing forward. This is the church of our Lord, our Savior, our Commanding Officer. We the church are still pushing forward on a relentless march for souls.

In the Spirit I had already seen massive demon strongholds which had formed around Grand Island, Nebraska, and I knew that it was up to me to break them up and send them scattering out of that region. I knew that if I didn't take charge of that situation, I would have lost many souls. Knowing then what I had to do meant I could not blame the Holy Spirit, my Senior partner. If I neglected to use my authority, I could only blame myself. I had to cast Satan out of the region. I had to tell Satan that this crusade was ordered by the courts of heaven who has also authorized me as the Captain of this crusade under Christ's authority to take charge.

My mission was to bring as many souls as I could into the Kingdom of God. I therefore commanded Satan not to interfere. I also commanded him not to interfere with all those souls who wanted to come. Not to cause any diversions or arguments, or financial hardships, or to develop unfortunate circumstances. I also told Satan, that authority was given to me by Christ Jesus, the one who won the ultimate battle of the Universe against him. That I cover Grand Island with Christ's blood, so I can present Christ the hope of glory to the people of this region. My authority was standing in the name of Jesus Christ, King of the seen and the unseen forces around us. Millions of celestial soldiers [unseen by the naked eye] with chariots of fire were standing in the wings to ensure that Satan obeyed my command to stay away until my mission was successfully accomplished. This was possible for me to do because God is no respecter of persons. God's Word will accomplish what it is sent to accomplish. When a child of God, any child of God acts on His Word, that word goes to accomplish. It will perform for you and me just as if it was God himself who spoke it.

Satan had no option but to obey, because of the power Jesus gave me, which was the same power He gave the seventy disciples,

> And the seventy returned again with joy, saying Lord, even the devils are subject to us through thy name. And He said unto them, I beheld Satan as lightning falling from heaven. Behold, I give unto you power to tread on serpents and scorpions, and over all the power of the enemy: and nothing shall by any means hurt you.
>
> Luke 10:17–19

By the time we landed the plane at the little airport in Grand Island, Nebraska, I was ready to preach. Pastor Arny and Dexter were there to meet us. They had set up five hundred chairs in the hall at the race course. Everything was in place and Pastor Arny's church was going to take care of the music. By the time we got started that evening, every one of the five hundred chairs in the meeting hall had someone sitting in them. It was obvious that between the Lord and Dexter, they did a fantastic job. Pastor Arny assured me that his church had done intercessory prayer for the crusade. In my spirit eye, I could see Satan sitting high and dry on a hilltop somewhere, and all he could do was watch and chew on his finger nails. I said to myself, "Tonight the blood of Jesus is going to freely flow one more time. Sinners stained by sin are going to be as white as snow at the end of the night." This was my biggest meeting to date to preach.

For three nights the services were filled and every night when I made the alter call the seats emptied with people standing a solid line against the walls. I had no idea how many got saved, or how many were filled with the Holy Spirit. But one person I will never forget. A young girl of sixteen was standing in the line. When it was her turn to be prayed for, the Holy Spirit said to me, "The girl you are about to pray for is on drugs and needs deliverance." This where the Light shines into the darkness and the darkness can not hide from the Light. I said, "Young lady! Tonight Jesus wants to deliver you from drugs." Instantly she swung around and walked away. I had several hundred people waiting in line for prayer and continued praying, not knowing what happened to the sixteen year old girl until six months later when I met her again. Pastor Arny introduced her to me this time. She told me that at first she thought that her friend had told me about her drug problem. But when she went back to her seat, her friend denied that she mentioned anything to me. Her friend explained to her that it must have been the Holy Spirit who revealed the problem to me, because her friend said, "Jesus loves you and He wants to deliver you." Her friend prayed the prayer of salvation with her and she accepted Jesus as her Savior back in the seats. After the service was over she went home and shared Jesus with her family of sixteen brothers and sisters of which she was the youngest. Her entire family was in the drug business. Some of her brothers were in a continual battle with the law enforcement and at two occasions were involved in a shootout with the police. Very happy that she received salvation, she told me that Jesus saved and delivered each of forty members of her family over a six-month period. They were all together in the drug business and now they all served Jesus together. Over forty in all counting the in-laws, was now attending Pastor Arny's church.

As I listened to her testimony I realized that for the past

six months, Satan has been sitting on that hill, still counting his losses. All he could do was to watch in humiliation and agony as entire households were getting saved and the works of the Holy Spirit still in full swing six months later.

Things also changed for pastor Arny. All those people at the crusade saw pastor Arny at the crusade every night. They started to make contact with him after the crusade. Pastor Arny who was overjoyed to see so many souls saved, did not want to see them backslide back into Satan's traps. Pastor Arny knew there were other churches in the area who would love to have them, but his desire was for God to let him be a shepherd to them. He began to intercede for them, because he knew the road was steep and narrow. Without the teaching and guidance of a shepherd their fate could be determined by a merciless enemy who was just waiting for someone to fall. Pastor Arny asked God to give all the new sheep to him and when God did, pastor Arny's church with seating for eighty was too small. Six months later Pastor Arny had a flock of five to six hundred on Sunday mornings and they were having their Sunday services in the local school auditorium.

> And so were the churches established in faith, and increased in number daily.
>
> Acts. 16:5

Money for the Crusade

But my God shall supply all your need according to His riches in glory by Christ Jesus.

Philippians 4:19

This chapter on the Grand Island crusade would not be complete if I did not tell you how God provided the money to pay for the expenses of the crusade. I mentioned earlier how that several ministries tried to conduct a crusade and folded up half way and left without paying their debt.

The Friday night was the last night of the crusade and we did not take one offering during any of the meetings. I was still following the procedures I learned at the Morris Curello ministers workshop. But that Friday night, the last night of the crusade, I announced that I had set up a breakfast offering service for ten o'clock on that Saturday morning and invited all who would like to support my ministry to come. After the meeting that night I was standing at the door greeting the people as they were leaving. One by one as the people shook my hand and left, many said to me, "We really enjoyed the meetings, but this is Thanks Giving weekend, and my car is packed, my family and I are leaving for out of town. I am so sorry I would not be able to come to the breakfast offering."

Only a few said they would be come. My prayer that evening was, "Please God, I don't need any money out of this deal for myself. But please give me enough money to pay Dexter for the expenses of the crusade." Not much of a faith prayer I admit, but I would have been terribly embarrassed if I was unable to give Dexter the money for the crusade. Early that morning I was praying again to ask God to please send enough people to the breakfast with money to cover the cost of two thousand dollars. Then the Lord asked me, "How much was your cost?" I said, "Well Lord, you know, I have to give Dexter two thousand dollars for the advertising." "When you ask for an offering today." The Lord replied to me, "Ask for twelve thousand dollars." "Lord!" I said, "Twelve thousand dollars! I don't need that much. Besides, too few people are coming, it will be impossible to get twelve thousand dollars from them." Unimpressed with my unbelief the Lord said, "You need twelve thousand dollars, because you offered all the tapes of the crusade for free and you would have to send thousands of tapes out by mail. You are also going to have massive correspondence and other expenses which you are unaware of at this time and I don't want you to embarrass Myself by not being able to fulfill your promises."

Stunned, I just stood there for a while. The figure God gave me flashed before my eyes, twelve thousand dollars. Now that will be interesting to see the surprise on people's faces at the breakfast when I tell them what the Lord told me. That morning after the breakfast was over I stood up to tell the forty people that were there what God had said to me. I started out by saying, "God told me in prayer this morning that it will take twelve thousand dollars to cover to cost of this crusade." I waited for the words to take effect, I was waiting for whispers and words of disgust, like money-hungry preacher. But just then a man jumped to his feet and said, "The Lord told me to give you a thousand dollars." He no sooner sat down and another one stood up and another, and another and on and on. One lady who identified herself as the wife of the Attorney General, gave three thousand dollars. There were shouts of joy as the people themselves tallied the money. Some were giving praise testimonies. The Holy Spirit was in control. We were having a revival in the restaurant, the people who were there were rejoicing that their prayers, which they had prayed for many years had been answered. Every time someone stood up to tell what God had told them to give they would give a short testimony at the same time. Shouts of praise reverberated through the restaurant area where we had our meeting. God had delivered people from oppression and sickness and defeat. My spirit man was leaping on the inside of me, I was moved with too much emotion to say anything, all I could do was listen to the people who God had filled with overflowing joy. I did not want to leave. I did not want the meeting to end. Along with these believers I was basking in the presence of His glorious works.

This is what Calvary was all about. It still is about deliverance, and about new relationships forming between the Father and His children. It is about scoring victories over a defeated foe who would not be able to defeat that group of believers again. Because that day they also experienced the ultimate joy anyone can have on this earth. The fellowship of the King of Kings and the assurance that they are never alone. He is always there, right by their side, leading them one day at a time. The job God had in mind got done. Even as in this crusade, God had to use someone who was sent from Africa. God is faithful. At times it may seem that God did not hear our prayers. Doubt may begin to build as the enemy tries to flame those doubts. The Apostle Paul says,

"Let us hold fast the profession [confession] of our faith without wavering; for He is faithful that promised" (Hebrews 10:23).

When the meeting finally came to a close sometime in the afternoon, we counted the money and we had twelve thousand dollars. I gave Dexter his money and I said good-bye to a brother who had faith when no one else did. I also had a feeling that God had many blessings waiting for Dexter. But I had to go, after all I was still on earth. Tomorrow I had to preach at the church I was pastoring. Probably tomorrow no one at church will grasp the significance of the revival I just came from.

> Now unto Him that is able to do exceeding abundantly above all that we ask or think, according to the power that worketh in us, unto Him be the glory in the church by Christ Jesus through out ages, world without end.
>
> Ephesians 3:20, 21

This is God's Special Agent signing off, mission accomplished and a great thank you to my Senior partner, "The Holy Spirit." Remember, Satan is not in charge. The circumstance is not in charge. God has placed you in charge. My message for the church is plain and simple. God wants you. God loves you. God needs you. God has a job lined up just for you. Release your faith today and say, "God here I am if you can use me I am available." You could also become a *Secret Agent for God.* Learn to follow the Holy Spirit. God's promise to His children is,

> And Jesus said unto them, Because of your unbelief; for verily I say unto you, If ye have faith as a grain of mustard seed,

> ye shall say unto this mountain, Remove hence to yonder place; and it shall remove; and nothing shall be impossible.
>
> Matthew 17:20

Step out in faith today. Overrule your mind and decide to follow after the Holy Spirit. Don't be afraid to make a mistake. You can always repent from making a mistake. What we can't repent of is in the day of judgment when the Lord looks at you and says: "You did nothing! In that day no excuse will be acceptable.

> Then the king will say to those on His right hand, "Come, you blessed of My Father, inherit the kingdom prepared for you from the foundation of the world: for I was hungry and you gave Me to food; I was thirsty and you gave me drink; I was a stranger and you took Me in; I was naked and you clothed Me; I was sick and you visited Me; I was in prison and you came to Me." "Then the righteous will answer Him, saying, "Lord, when did we see You hungry and feed You, or thirsty and give You drink? "When did we see You a stranger and take You in, or naked and cloth You? , Or when did we see You sick, or in prison and come to You?, And the King will answer and say to them, Assuredly, I say to you, inasmuch as you did it to one of the least of these My bretheren, you did it to Me.
>
> Matthew 25:34–40, NKJV

God's Secret Agent

For it is not ye that speak, but the Spirit of your Father which speaketh in you.

Matthew 10:20

Now when they saw the boldness of Peter and John, and perceived that they were unlearned and ignorant men, they marveled; and they took knowledge of them, that they had been with Jesus.

Acts 4:13

God is still looking for men and women who are bold and unafraid, who are willing to go where ever it is the Spirit of God takes them. One Sunday after church on our way home, God gave me the strangest assignment of my life. There was a church organization who I was affiliated with. Even though I held my ordination papers with this organization, hardly any of their pastors would allow me to minister in their churches. One particular church was in the countryside in Arkansas, located in a farming community.

I wondered what the pastor of that church was afraid of

when he wrote me a letter that stated, "Unless you are willing to submit yourself to the elders of my church and attend my services for six months, I will not let you come and preach in my church." Short and to the point.

Several months had passed, when that Sunday on my way home from church the Lord said to me, "Call pastor Dan Kelly and tell him that you will preach in his church tonight." I thought, "Well, O.K. Lord, I wonder how he will respond to that."

The church of Dan Kelly was about a four hour drive from Tulsa. When I got home I called Dan, who I had never met before. The letter from me to him, and him to me had been the only contact with each other. When he answered the phone I said, "Pastor, this is Corrie Joubert in Tulsa, remember we wrote each other a few months back. God told me to preach in your church tonight, please give me directions how to get there?" After Dan gave me the directions, I said, "Dan God told me to be at your church and preach tonight. I will see you as soon as I get there." I said good-bye and hung up the phone, before Dan could object.

After I had lunch, I got into my car and left for Dan's church. The Lord told me to take a change of clothing since I would be there for several days. Of cause, Dan had no idea what was going down either. In the car going, I prayed for Dan to be obedient to whatever it was God had in store for him that day. Usually when God sent one of His disciples on a secret mission like this, only He knew what was going to happen. The disciple [me] stays informed only on a need to know basis. The operation will go off in secret, and me, the disciple operates by mustard seed faith. I know that God has everything completely under His control and that there was no force between heaven and earth powerful enough to interfere. That way, even God's and our enemy the Devil also don't know what is in the works. All Satan could do was summon his demons to watch and report every move I make. While Satan himself is walking around roaring like a toothless lion. Through my spirit eye I could visualize what was taking place in the world of fallen spirits and what I saw gave me immeasurable pleasures. In fact I was overjoyed. Every time God sends me on a mission to erode Satan's power over God's people and to set His children free, I feel nothing but joy!

I could imagine that Satan by now was in conference with his demons trying to inquire what was going down. Unfortunately for Satan, his demons did not know either. The information was secret and God was the only one who knew.

I had an inkling that night, that people were going to bathe in the precious blood of Jesus, while others will be wrapped in His stripes for cleansing and healing. Demons who had kept some of God's precious children in fear and bondage would have to flee that church screaming with torment as they count their losses.

The moment my car stopped in front of Pastor Dan's house, he came out, not to greet me but to tell me, "Brother Corrie, I will let you preach, since you have come all this way. But don't expect an offering. I don't take up offerings for preachers who invite themselves." I said; "Brother Dan that's O.K. You see God always takes care of me." I went into the church to wait for the meeting to start. While Pastor Dan went back inside his house. It was obvious that we had nothing pleasant to say to each other.

When the service started I was surprise to see a little country church packed to capacity. After a few dry songs and ritualistic solemn prayers, the pastor introduced me and gave me the mike. With great enthusiasm I began to share how good God was, and how present His Spirit was, and how God was there in our midst just waiting to pull someone closer to Him. I began to share how God had healed a man in a crusade in Rapid City South Dakota who had been on a dialysis machine for twelve years. The night that God gave him two new kidneys, he went home to drink all the water he was not able to drink all those years. I also shared about the lady who came to a meeting with water on her lungs, she had to make regular visits to the clinic to have the water drained. That night she came to my meeting she could not speak over a whisper. Because of the water on her lungs. During the service God healed her and when I asked for testimonies she was the first to jump up to testify. The water did not only drain from her lungs, but she was able to talk so loud, she did not even need a mike.

Every one in Dan's church was listening intensely. Some sitting on the edge of their pew, when the Holy Spirit started to move. God had me point to a sister and say to her, "The Lord said you have been yearning to be used by the Holy Spirit and bring a message in tongues. Stand up, this moment, the Lord releases you from your fears. Now stand up on your feet and give that message in tongues."The words in an unknown tongue came bellowing out of her mouth. Then the Lord had me point at a another Lady and say to her, "The Lord says that you have been yearning in your heart to interpret tongues in this church, but there are never any tongues to interpret. The Lord said tonight, you interpret the message in tongues that was just given." The sister stood up, and interpret for the first time in her life. Her message was to her pastor, she said, "Tonight the Lord floods your church with living waters, and tonight the Lord delivers you from fear."

After a couple more tongues and interpretations, the Lord began to pour healing on a few folks. It was great, the church could not remember when last the Spirit of the Lord had moved in that church. You see, Dan was always afraid that something will get out of control and then God will blame him. But that night, Pastor Dan saw for himself that God's Spirit will also control those who he chooses to use.

After the meeting was over and many of the people had said how much they enjoyed the meeting, Pastor Dan came to me and said, "You know I told you that I don't take offerings for ministers who invite themselves. Well, I am sorry I said that, and here is a hundred dollars. It did not come out of the offering. A man of my church gave me two hundred dollars, he said one hundred for you for getting tonights speaker and one hundred for the speaker." Pastor Dan also apologized for his attitude and said he was glad that God overruled him.

By now the demons were going crazy, trying to see what they could do for damage control. But God was not through yet. The Pastor said, "Brother Corrie please stay tonight; tomorrow we will go and visit some other folks." A good thing that the Lord already prepared me to stay.

I had to stay in the children's bedroom, while the children slept in the living room. Just as I came out of my room the next morning, the phone rang. It was around 8:00 or 8:30. The conversation was short. When Pastor Dan put the phone down he said, "That was one of my church members. He recently broke his ankle, he is a professional football player. His doctor told him when he broke his foot that he will not be able to play for the rest of the season. Last night in the service he had a warm sensation going from his foot up his leg. When that happened he knew that God had healed his foot. He has just come from his doctors office, where he had the doctor up and in his office early this morning. They took x-ray's at his insistence and could find no trace of a break. He said that the doctor has just cleared him to go back to his game today."

Now probably none of this would have happened if God had to wait for Dan to invite me to his Church. But wait, the miracle was still in progress. The Lord said, "Ask Dan to help you put a crusade together." Whoops! I said, "Lord, have you seen how small this town is? If you blink you can miss it." "Yes, and that is why I want you to come." God said, "You see the big boys won't come here, but you will, that is why I am asking you." God is so good to me all the time, I just have to go on and do whatever it is He wants me to do even if I don't understand why. Two months later our crusade started in that little town of only a couple of hundred residents. That would be counting the farmers and the town folks. For the size of the town we had a remarkable turnout. We were using the school gymnasium and had from eighty to a hundred people. Daily Pastor Dan and I would go to the hill, a steep hill with a radio tower on it. That hill was the highest point overlooking the town and we would go there daily to pray over the town. We would stretch our hands towards the town and ask God to save souls and set people free from bondage.

I knew Satan was doing everything he could to conjure up something so he could interrupt the meetings. When the first night a bunch of demons got into the sound equipment, I knew that God was about to do something wonderful. The volume was so high, it almost blasted the people out the door. I kept signaling to the brother at the controls to turn down the sound, and the more he turned the sound down, the louder it became. So he turned it off. It was still too loud; he then unplugged it and it was still too loud. Then we stopped what we were doing, gathered a few believers around the equipment laid hands on it and commanded Satan to get out. After the prayer we turned the equipment back on and it worked perfect Praise God . . .

Sometimes one wonders why Satan "doesn't just give it up! He must know that we know that greater is He that is in me, than he that is in the world.

Two days before the meetings were over the Lord said to

me, "I am going to give you a financial miracle of twenty-five thousand dollars out of this crusade, but before I can give you the money, you must ask Dan if he minds. In fact you have to get him to agree with you in prayer for the twenty-five thousand dollars, before I can give it to you, because after this crusade I will give Dan a Miracle." [We did not know it at the time, but about a year later God allowed Dan to move on with the people in his church who hungered for more. Dan and his new group was able to build a brand new church for cash, and God filled his church with many new people.] That day when we were back on top of the hill to pray I said, "Dan, the Lord wants to give me a financial miracle in this crusade. I want to know how you would feel about that." Dan said, "It won't bother me, but you have not even taken an offering yet, how will God give you a financial miracle?"

I replied, "The way we will do that is, I will announce at the meetings that anyone who feels led of God to give anything to my ministry will meet Saturday after the crusade for a separate breakfast meeting. That way, only the persons who feel led of God to give will be there." Pastor Dan replied, "That is just fine brother Corrie, but I can tell you right now, that this is a very poor community. Don't expect much." I said, "Pastor Dan, have faith, God knows how much money is here." "Well brother Corrie, he said, "did God also tell you how much that offering will be?" I said, "Yes He did, and I will tell you only if you promise not to get mad, because you see, if you unselfishly allow God to do this for me. You on the other hand open yourself to get even a bigger blessing from God." Dan thought about what I said for a minute and replied, "I will not get mad, tell me how much." I said, "Twenty-five thousand dollars." Pastor Dan just sat there for a while in silence. I sat in silence with him, I knew that the Holy Spirit was ministering to him. When he spoke he said, "Brother Corrie, if God give you twenty-five thousand dollars it would have to be a miracle. Because I don't think that there is twenty-five thousand dollars in this county." "But," he said, "I will be glad to agree with you."

Saturday morning during the offering breakfast, forty people in total showed up. After we had our coffee and dough nuts. We opened with prayer and I said, "The Lord wants to give my ministry twenty-five thousand dollars today. I want each person who God had already told what to give to stand up and say what God had told you to give." Three people stood up almost simultaneously, Dan the Pastor was the first, said, "The Lord told me to give five thousand." The second brother said, "The Lord told me to give five thousand." The third brother said, "The Lord wants me to give five thousand." Then others stood up and in about fifteen minutes when everyone had said what the Lord had told them to give, we totaled it all up and it came to twenty-five thousand dollars.

God that day dispelled all Pastor Dan's fears. [1] Dan's fear that there was no money in that county. [2] The fear that the Spirit of the Lord could not be trusted to lead all the church services. [3] The fear of not belonging to an organization. No minister of God needs to be in bondage to a denomination that restricts the moving of the Holy Ghost in the church. Just let God reign in your life.

Soon after that crusade, Dan took the people of God in the church he was pastoring, the ones who wanted to grow and move forward and separated from the denominational church. To his utter surprise God pulled together a group of believers that build a church twice the size of the old one for cash. And filled up the church with a lot of new people.

Fellow believer, you too can become a member of God's secret service. You can commit yourself to take a stand for the kingdom of God and make a public display of Satan. Let people around you know that greater is He that is in you, than he that is in the world. By now we all realize that every time a believer gives Satan a blow to the head, that he is going to retaliate. If your fear of Satan is greater than your trust in God, Satan will continue to keep you in bondage.

A few weeks later I had gone to a meeting and a friend had taken me in his plane. On our way back to Tulsa something happened to the plane. We were crossing the river and in the distance we could already see the airport. When all of a sudden the engine stopped. No matter how the pilot tried, he could not get the engine to start again. He said to me "Pray, we are going to crash, the airport is still too far to reach." We prayed and asked the Holy Spirit to take control of the plane. The pilot tried again to start the plane, and that time it started. We landed safely on the landing strip.

The next day when the mechanics pulled the engine out to see what went wrong they found that a broken piston had gone through the block of the engine. That would have made it impossible for the engine to run. But they that are for us are more than they that are against us. If we truly belief that nothing is impossible. If only we had faith like Elisha and could see into the spirit world, has been my prayer. With God nothing, absolutely nothing is impossible.

One day, a month or so after the crusade, I was at the car wash when the attendant called me. When I walked into the office he handed me the phone. When I answered it was Genny, she said there were some people from Arkansas that has driven four hours to see me and wanted to know if I could come home immediately. During the month after the crusade the twenty-five thousand dollars had been coming in payments as people were able to fulfill their commitments. There was one man I had not heard from and when I walked into the house it was he and his wife. He had a big smile on his face. After we greeted he gave me a cashiers check. I was surprised when I saw that it contained his total pledge of five thousand dollars. Jokingly I said, "Brother did you rob a bank." To which he replied, "This is the biggest blessing of my life. You see I had a piece of land that I have tried to sell for years, but no one even wanted to give me five thousand dollars for it. A week after I made the pledge which I know God told me to make. There was a knock on my door about eight one morning. When I opened the door to see who it was, I saw a stranger I had never seen before. He asked me if that was my property and if it was for sale, referring to the property I have been unable to sell. I said yes it was mine and it was for sale. The man then said he will pay me fifteen thousand dollars cash that day if I would sell it to him, but not one penny more. Of course, I immediately accepted his offer. You see the Lord not only gave me the five thousand dollars for my pledge, but he also gave me an extra five thousand for myself over and above what I thought the property was worth."

I could see why the brother was so happy. He learned that it was impossible to out give God.

> For in Christ Jesus you are all sons of God, through faith. For as many of you who were baptized into Christ have put on Christ. There is neither Jew nor Greek, there is neither slave nor free, there is neither male nor female: for you are all one in Christ Jesus. And if you are Christ's, then you are Abraham's offspring, heirs according to the promise.
>
> Galatians 3:26–29, RSV

Once a child of God *is* clothed with Christ, then that child becomes completely invisible to Satan. Satan then no longer knows who is in that clothing. All Satan really sees is a lot of Jesus' walking around. The only way he could ever know you are the one in that covering, is when he hears doubt coming from your confession. But all the time while you speak God's word to the problem, not your word, not your assessment, not your fears. No all you speak to the problem is what the word of God has to say about the problem. Then you exercise the authority of the word of God, and the word of God will always accomplish.

Neither you nor I can ever be good enough to earn this kind of favor from God. But in all our short comings, we have been adopted by our heavenly Father. Now all that belongs to Jesus, also belongs to us. So, go ahead! Call God Daddy. Call God Father, because you are His child through the new birth experience. And in faith by accepting His forgiveness, you also accept His adoption, becoming His Son.

> I have been crucified with Christ [that really means I share His crucifixion, accepting the fact that Jesus paid my debt] it is no longer I who live [no longer the sinful old me] but Christ who lives in me, [now all my imperfections is covered with Christ] and the life I now live in the flesh, [that old weak, fearful, doubtful, can't get it right, that me] I live by the faith of the Son of God, who loved me and gave Himself for me. [By faith Christ did what I could not do, He paid my debt, knowing that I am weak and imperfect. He went ahead and covered me in His righteousness, thus, all my imperfections are now covered over, so Satan can't see me, all he can see is Jesus.]
>
> Galatians 2:20, RSV

Casting a Demon Out of a Girl

> There came a certain man, kneeling down to Him, and saying, Lord, have mercy on my son: for he is a lunatic, and sore vexed: for oftimes he falleth and oft into the water. And Jesus rebuked the devil; and he departed out of him: and the child was cured from that hour.
>
> Matthew 17:14,18

I was pastoring a small denominational church. About one year earlier when I met the group, they only had eight people left in the church. But this Sunday one year later, the church was filled with well over a hundred worshipers. After I gave the Sunday message, which was coordinated with the taking of communion, I offered anyone who had something in their hearts that needed forgiveness, an opportunity to pray. I also asked if there was anyone who needed to come and pray at the altar to come forward. Two ladies came. One came for salvation and I prayed with her to receive Jesus. The other young lady who came to the front also knelt at the altar. I started to go down and meet her to pray with her. But the Holy Spirit stopped me and said, "Don't touch her, she has a evil spirit. The name of the spirit is xxxxxx. Call him out of her."

In obedience to the Holy Spirit I then proceeded to call the spirit by his name and commanded him to come out of her. Suddenly the girl at the altar stiffened and fully stretched out with her body in a horizontal position, began to rise from the floor and remained levitated for a few seconds and then dropped. She fell onto the floor stomach down with a thud. I followed the same procedure three times calling the evil spirit by his name and every time the same thing happened. However, the third time I called the spirit to come out, the spirit came out of her. The moment he let her go she became relaxed and in control of her movements, and she was able to kneel again.

By this time most of the worshipers in the church who had never seen Satan manifesting his evil powers in that particular fashion were sitting on the edge of their pews. Terrified some got up and walked out.

After the evil spirit released the girl, we continued and served communion. The rest of the service went without any further incidence. However, after the service was over, the elder of the church who was there when I first met the group, called me to the side and said, "I am very displeased with your performance today. I had some friends in the church and you terrified the congregation today. You should have waited until after the service to exorcise the spirit out of the girl, not have done it in front of the congregation."

I tried to tell him that I had to do what I did when the Holy Spirit said to do it. He however was not in agreement and asked me not to come back. Six months later the church was back to their original eight. They decided to join-up with another congregation and the church was shut down. "If you are reproached for the name of Christ, you are blessed, for the spirit of glory and of God rests upon you" (1 Peter 4:14, RSV).

Principles of the Invisible Kingdom

The Laws And The By-laws For The Family Business: The Minimum Required Standards to Qualify for The New Covenant Blessings:

Therefore if thine enemy hunger, feed him; if he thirst, give him a drink: for in so doing thou shalt heap coals of fire on his head. Be not overcome with evil, but overcome evil with good.

Romans 12:20–21

The following interpretation of the sermon on the mount as it was given by Jesus is not a literal interpretation and should not be regarded as such. The author simply wishes to draw attention to its importance. It's my sincere desire to see more of God's children take these instructions given by Jesus serious. The way I have interpreted the sermon, simply projects my own personal understanding of the sermon by Jesus. I suggest, that believers prayerfully asks the Holy Spirit to illuminate the scripture, to grasp the full meaning of the importance of the sermon on the mount. Not understanding the importance of what Jesus is saying could mean the difference in experiencing a meaningful relationship with the Father, or constantly wondering, why God is not answering your prayers.

Taken from the Sermon on the Mount
Jesus said; Matthew chapter five.

1. verse 3 | Blessed are the poor in spirit, [Humble/Broken] for theirs is the kingdom of heaven. [In essence, they will enjoy the benefits of the invisible kingdom now.] [Also see Psalm 51:17, Isa. 57:16. 61:2.].
2. verse 4 | Blessed are they that mourn. [Express sorrow for something regrettable, like past sins, a penitent spirit] for they shall be comforted. [They will experience the joy of a new life in Christ.] [Isa. 61:2.]
3. verse 5 | Blessed are the meek. [Patient and long suffering, those who do not to take retribution in their own hands, but let God deal with it, a mild tempered gentle spirit. Someone who does not think that he/she is better than anyone else.] For they shall inherit the earth. [God will supply their needs under the blessings of the new covenant, like in the case of Abraham.][Also see Ps. 37:11 and 1 Peter 3:8]
4. verse 6 | Blessed are they which do hunger and thirst after righteousness: [Strive to know God's word and make every effort to remain in right standing with God.] for they shall be filled. [They will walk in the new covenant blessings which includes power to cast out devils. Heal the sick. They acknowledge that God is their source. They will feed the hungry, cloth the naked and house the homeless.] [Also see: Ps. 34:10; 42:1–3; 63:1; 84:2; John 7:37–39.]
5. verse 7 | Blessed are the merciful: [Being lenient, like when someone owes you money and can't pay, you are willing to go the second mile, or forgive the debt. Full of compassion and

mercy] for they shall obtain mercy. [God will also go easy on you.] [See also 1 Peter 3:8–11]

6. verse 8 | Blessed are the pure in heart: [People who don't hold grudges, forgives easily, full of love, free from sin, stands faultless and blameless before God. Washed! in the blood of Jesus.] For they shall see God. [Without a doubt they will one day be with God in heaven.] [Also see Philippians 4:8]
7. verse 9 | Blessed are the peacemakers: [Without conflict or hostility. One who does not look for faults in others. Even if others regard him as a enemy, he/she returns love and try to look for the good in the other person. Offers wisdom and mediation] For they shall be called the children of God. [Sons of God. A member of God's family having full rights to come boldly in His presence at any time.] [Also see Romans 14:19; 1 Cor. 13.]
8. verse10–13 | Blessed are they which are persecuted for righteousness sake: [When your relationship with the Father is misunderstood by others. When they call you names and accuse you falsely.] For theirs is the kingdom of heaven. [Those are the kind of people who will definitely live with God in heaven one day.] [Also see 1 Peter 3:14–16; 4:3–19.] Blessed are ye, when men shall revile you, and persecute you, and shall say all manner of evil against you falsely, for my sake. Rejoice, and be exceeding glad: for great is your reward in heaven: for so persecuted they the prophets which were before you. [You should consider it an honor when people speak evil of you and slander your name, in fact it is a blessing in disguise, they are actually doing you a favor, don't retaliate, because when you don't allow it to affect your spirit, your heavenly father will reward you in ways you never imagined].[Acts 5:4; 16:25, 1 Peter 4:13.]

Instead of quoting the Bible verse first, from this point on I will just give you my personal interpretation, please read on. The actual scripture verse will appear at the end of each section.

You are the salt of the earth, don't follow the crowd. As a child of God you should be a leader instead, imparting to others the values of the invisible kingdom. [Verses 13]

Shine your light so the crowd will follow you. Live your life by example, so others will look at you and realize that living in God's invisible kingdom is the real thing. [Verses 14–16]

God did not do away with the principles of the ten commandments, they are to remain in full force. The rules of the kingdom has not changed any at all. I merely want to elaborate on it's importance, and don't you try to change them either. As a matter of fact, they will remain in force as long as there is a heaven and a earth. Only people who wants to remain on the bottom of the ladder will attempt to change any thing. The secret to moving up the ladder in God's kingdom is to comply and to tell others to comply also. [Verses 17–19]

I am not looking for self righteous people, but for followers with pure hearts. [Verse 20]

Offer forgiveness readily at all times, never take matters into your own hands. In fact the truth is that God doesn't even want you to be angry with anyone at any time. Don't ever get into a full blown argument with anyone at any time and risk your right standing with God. Its just not worth it. That also means that when you come to church and wants to place your gift to God in the offering plate and remembers that you still have a unresolved argument on your hands. Leave the meeting and go to nearest phone and call that person and forgive them, than come back and place your gift in the offering plate. [Verses 21–24]

Always take care of your responsibilities. Remain on good

terms with anyone you indebted to. Don't wait until someone is ready to drag you into court, by than it is to late. [Verses 25–26]

Don't get caught up into looking for a better spouse in someone else and risk falling into sin. Even entertaining such a thought is already considered sinful. [Verses 27–28]

If the circumstances surrounding you cause you to sin, change the circumstance. If it is a job change the job. If it is family and friends than move on. What ever it is, is not worth risking your right standing with the Father. [Verses 29–30]

Never use divorce as the easy way out, instead apply the above principles. You don't want to be the one that have to be accountable for causing her/him to sin. [Verses 31–32]

Be a person of your word. Always do what you say, so others will know that they can always count on you. God also wants you to be a person of integrity. [Verse 33–37]

The world wants what's theirs and more, even if they have to take you to court. You don't have to be like them. Give them what they want, its just not worth fighting over. Even if they take advantage of you, don't worry. Let people take advantage of you, If they take your pay check for example, ask them if they would like to go with you and get a bite to eat. Also when someone wants to borrow from you. Go ahead help them all you can. [Verses 38–42]

The world only love those who loves them, but God expects you to love even your enemies. No matter how unfair someone has been towards you in the past, still help that person if they asks you. Be like your Father, He treats them good, even when they did not deserve it. So God expect you to do the same, in that way you presents the same kind of image for the family business as your Father. [Verses 43–48]

Continuing the Principles of the Invisible Kingdom

Matthew Chapter Six

The following is the author's own
interpretation of Matthew chapter six.

When you give to God or help others, don't go around bragging about it. For those who always broadcast every little thing they do, already received their reward. Give in secret, your Father who knows what you gave will than reward you openly. [Verse 1–4]

Don't only pray in church, also pray at home by yourself, just talking to your Father in private prayer, one on one. Remember, it is not how much you pray about the same thing that counts, or how loud you shout, pray in faith and trust your Father for the answer, He will reward you openly. [Verses 5–8]

The Model Prayer Matthew 6:9–13.

My Father in heaven, I bless your holy name.

Allow Your kingdom to operate on earth as it operates in heaven.

Supply all my needs for this day.

Forgive me of all my sins in the same way as I forgive others of their sins.

Help me not to fall into temptation, but deliver me from sinful circumstances.

For the kingdom here on earth is also Yours, and all the power and the glory.

Prayer without forgiveness is pointless. You may as well not even bother to pray. As God forgives you when you falter and fall, so He expects you to forgive others their faults. Otherwise you will not be forgiven either. [Verses 14–15]

When you fast or intercede in prayer, do it joyfully, dress up and cheerfully go about your business. No one but your Father even needs to know what you are doing. [Verses 16–18]

Don't compete with the world to see how successful you can be, worldly success is not worth a thing. Rather, see what you can accomplish in God's invisible kingdom, [The family business] for which your Father will reward you handsomely. [Verses 19–21]

It is impossible to compete in the world system and build the family business at the same time. You have a choice, either build with the world, or build the family business with your Father. [Verses 22–24]

When you are in the family business with your Father, you don't have to worry about your own business or job. You see, God our Father takes good care of His responsibilities. Take for instance the things in nature like flowers and birds. If God can take care of the planet, surely, He can also take care of you while you building the family business with Him. I suggest you don't even give the Fathers love and ability to care for you a second thought, just trust Him. Often people are to concerned with their daily needs for food and clothing, paying their light bill etc. . But your heavenly Father wants you to know that, that kind of anxiety is unnecessary. If you can only learn to trust Him, you will realize just how well He will take care of you, on your job, in your business, in your family life. Fear belongs to the unredeemed, it certainly should not have any hold on God's own family members who has been redeemed from the curse. [Verses 25–34.]

Continuing the Principles of the Invisible Kingdom

Matthew Chapter Seven

"Be very careful in judging how well or poorly others perform, God has not engaged you to critique others. In God's kingdom one is usually judged by God with the same measure you use to judge others with. The best thing you can do is not to look for others faults, simply overlook them. Don't even try to propagate your excellent ideas to people who did not ask you for your opinion in the first place, offering your ideas to them would be a waste of your time. Besides even though you are a member of God's family, you still have faults of your own and have not reached perfection. Allow God to deal with the faults of the world and with yours. Basically the only person you need to concern yourself with is you and thus allow God to build your character. [Verses 1–6]

In this life if you want something you ask for it. Keep looking until you find what you are looking for. Keep knocking on doors until you find one that opens for you. You already know how earthly parents only want the best for their children. How much more do you think your Heavenly Father wants to give only good gifts to His family on earth. But you must take into account the laws and the by-laws of the invisible kingdom, that was placed into effect by God Himself through the Prophets. Treat others always in the exact same way you want your heavenly Father to treat you. [Verses 7–12]

But be careful to follow exactly the guidelines in your covenant manual. Many people feel that they can live however they want to, that is not true. You see, in all fairness, God will only honor the requests of those who strictly follow these rules. Learn the rules and live by them. [Verses 13–14]

Beware of people who come up with new ideas about how to serve God and build the family business. If you believe them, you will regret it. A good rule to go by will be to do a proper background check to assure they are on the up and up. Cross check scripture references they quote for yourself. When a preacher offers radical ideas, if it does not measure up with what Jesus had said in the laws of the invisible kingdom, you will be best served if you don't get involved. Every person who claims to be called of God as a manager [in the five fold ministry] must produce proof by the way they instruct their followers in building the invisible kingdom. You see, there are some preachers who are in this business for themselves, not for the family, don't allow them to deceive you. The day is coming when God will judge their works. They will still be standing there with their hand out, even trying to bluff the Father, lying about how hard they worked. But you see, God will simply say, "Sorry folks your time of deception ends here, you have never really helped to build the family business, so leave! I don't ever want to see you again." [Verses 15–23]

Now listen up close; As the representative of my Father, My advise to you is to pay close attention to the directions you received from Me today. Follow the instructions I gave you today, because it is your insurance policy to be productive in building the family business, which is the invisible kingdom. If you follow my directions, I assure you that your heavenly Father will take good care of you. You will overcome any obstacle the enemy throws in your way. But if you disregard my advice to you, you will certainly regret the outcome. Because you see, when the enemy throws obstacles in the way of those who don't follow the guidelines, they will face their problem without any help from God and be out in the cold by themselves." [Verses 24–27]

And God Said, And I Said, And Satan Said

> And the Lord God commanded the man saying, 'of every tree of the garden thou mayest freely eat: But of the tree of the knowledge of good and evil, thou shalt not eat. For in the day that thou eatest thereof thou shalt surely die. Genesis 2:16–17.
>
> Now the serpent was more subtle than any beast of the field which the Lord God had made. And he said unto the woman, Yea, hath God said, Ye shall not eat of every tree of the garden? And the woman said unto the serpent: We may eat of the trees of the fruit of the garden: But of the fruit of the tree which is in the midst of the garden, God hath said, Ye shall not eat of it, neither shalt thou touch it, lest ye die. And the serpent said unto the woman: Ye shall not surely die.
>
> Genesis 3:1–4

Let's stop and take a good look at what had just happened. I want to paint you a picture of today's church. If Christ had to stand in the pulpit today, *Jesus might say this,* "I have given you God's word in the sermon on the mountain, all you have to do is trust God and be about the family business as I was." You see,

God your Father's goal at this time, is to redeem the human race from the curse that came on them since Adam and Eve. The sermon on the mount is the policies and procedure manual to you, with directions on how we accomplish this task and share our Father's goal.

The Devil says, "Do you believe that stuff? Man you better believe if someone don't pay me what they owe me or someone mistreat my kid, I will see him in court. Do you see all those sorry looking people living in the street, and I must feed them and help them? Forget that, no one is stopping them from getting a job. If I have to work for a living, so can they."

You say, "Well, God did say in his word that we should feed the hungry and lend to those who ask us, and I want to do the right thing, I don't want to live under the curse any longer."

Satan says, "You know what, God don't expect you to do it, that is why we have a welfare system in this country. If God wanted you to do it, He would not have provided the welfare system."

You say, "Yes you know what, that makes perfect sense to me. I think I will do just that. I will let the government take care of them, then I will have more time for myself. And I will also pray for them, yes, that's what I will do, I will pray for the needy."

But you better watch out. If you believe that lie from Satan, you have done exactly what Adam and Eve did. That is good to pray for the needy, but we have to do a lot more than pray. We must do the job at hand, for if we do, we will experience God's abundance in our own lives. I believe the reason there are so many sorry, sick and poverty stricken Christians today, is simply because too many have not taken the word of God seriously.

Being Redeemed from the Curse!

Listen to what God said to Israel, my interpretation from the book of Deuteronomy chapter 28. I will quote the verses by number.

1. This is what you can expect to receive if you are willing to take God at His word and follow His instructions.
2. God will bless you more than you can imagine, if you just do what He says.
3. It would not matter if you live in the city, or in a rural area.
4. God will bless you with children and He will bless your livestock to multiply.
5. Whatever products you produce will be blessed, even if you run a business.
6. No matter what you undertake, you will be blessed.
7. If anyone opposes you, God will take care of the situation for you, so you don't have to worry.
8. God will command His blessings to come on you no matter what you undertake.
9. If you will only follow my instructions to you, God said, so I can be proud of you.
10. Then all the people in the world will know that I am your God. They will even be afraid to mess with you.

11. God will make you so rich with things, and children, and livestock, and in farming, and all this will happen on the property God gave you.
12. It will feel to you that the windows of heaven are simply pouring all God's blessings on you. You will be rich enough to lend to other nations.
13. God will make you the head of all your operations; you won't have to work for anyone. But all of this can only take place if you strictly follow God's guidelines.
14. You must follow God's instructions; it is in your best interest.
15. But if you disregard God's instructions, you will be on your own and you won't like what will happen to you. However, it can only happen if you disregard God's instructions to you.
16. You will open yourself up for all kinds of calamities.
17. You will be so bad off, you will accumulate debts all over the place.
18. Your children, your livestock and farming operations will be nothing but trouble.
19. It would not matter what you do, it will end up in disaster.
20. God would be unable to protect you from yourself. Sickness and disaster and ulcers will eat you up. You will be too miserable to live with yourself.
21. If you ran a farming operation you would constantly have to deal with every kind of insect and disease.
22. You will face problems like incurable diseases, with inflammation and fever, extreme heat, mildew, problems with your neighbors. It will feel at times that no matter what you do you are unable to get ahead.

23. You will feel alone and abandoned, even your prayers will go unanswered.
24. Even the elements will be against you and you will experience droughts, floods, and extreme heat.
25. No matter how nice you are or how hard you work, someone will always be there to oppose you and take from you.
26. You will develop illnesses that are incurable.
27. You will develop all kinds of diseases for which no cures can be found.
28. People will develop heart problems and nervous conditions, some will go blind, others will go crazy.
29. By noon you will already feel too tired to work, but would have to continue your day having this tired stupor feeling.
30. The woman you married as your wife will get tired of your incompetence and find herself someone else. Divorce will be the norm.
31. Farmers will really find it difficult with fluctuating prices and unstable markets. There will always be someone who will undercut and undermine you.
32. Children especially will find themselves in foster care or in single-parent family situations. But you will have such a difficult time making a living that even though your heart aches for them, there will be little you can do to change the situation.
33. At times you will get the feeling that whatever you do is in vain.
34. You will continuously be in a bad mood and develop bad eye sight.

35. You will develop problems in your legs and arms and sores on your skin.
36. All this will happen when you don't follow God's direction and refuse to put Him first.
37. In fact you will become the laughing stock of the world.
38. You will continuously be unsuccessful in your endeavors.
39. You will have to work for others, unable to enjoy.
40. Others will live in luxury, but you in poverty.
41. Your own children will take no notice of you. They will do whatever they want even to the point of embarrassing you.
42. There will be bugs every where.
43. You will even observe foreigners doing better financially than you are.
44. To get ahead and to stay on your feet, you will always have to borrow.

Do you see a pattern here? Are these not many of the things we see in our society today? Is this a picture of our American society? But just because we are all born under the curse does not mean that we have to stay there.

Jesus tells us in Matthew 6:33, *"But seek ye first the kingdom of God and His righteousness; and all these things shall be added unto you."* The principle: put God first!

Paul says in Romans 6:11, *"Likewise reckon ye also yourselves to be dead indeed to sin, but alive unto God through Jesus Christ our Lord."* Alive to God means that your communication has been re-established.

Romans 6:16 says, *"Know ye not that to whom ye yield yourselves servants to obey; whether of sin unto death, or of obedience unto righteousness."* If you follow the directions Christ Jesus gave, you have life. "The God kind of life" But if you follow the normal pattern, like everyone else, you will stay dead and not even know it. But Paul also holds out hope for us to change the circumstances in which we find ourselves, advising us to allow the Holy Spirit free access to accomplish God's work in us. Romans 8:11: "But if the same Spirit of Him that raised up Jesus from the dead dwell in you, He that raised up Christ from the dead shall also quicken your mortal bodies by the spirit that dwelleth in you."

God through the miracle of the new birth also infused your spirit with the same spirit that was in Jesus Christ and give you the ability to do supernatural miracles. Jesus reveals further that now as a member of the family of God, we have unlimited potential to turn the curse away from us and enjoy God's blessings. How? By taking responsibility for what we say and how we say it. By being in agreement with our heavenly Father.

The following is my interpretation of Mark 11: 22–26: Jesus said you must have faith in God. If you do, then you can say to your problem, any problem, big or small, "Go away! I don't want to see you any more."

All you have to do is to believe that your words are powerful and irrevocable. Once you said it, it will happen, exactly as you said it. If it was a negative confession you will get something negative, if it was a positive confession than you will get something good.

But you must realize that for your words to yield that kind of positive power you need to have a forgiving heart and not hold unforgiveness. With a clean and forgiving heart, God can endorse your words to be productive. Giving you all the things you believe for.

Jesus also tells us in Matthew 12:33–37 that once you are a part of the God family and you are working just as hard as you can in the family business, which is winning souls, you will be productive in doing good things.

However, you are surrounded by snakes and vipers who continue in their evil doings, talking like fools. But, you see, a good person is one who accepted God's way over his own and becomes very productive. However, an evil person is one who stubbornly continues to think he knows what he is doing. But don't you worry about a thing. They will be judged by their useless unproductive behavior and you will receive God's stamp of approval as you help Him build the kingdom.

Ask yourself this question: "Why was it necessary for Jesus to redeem you and me from the curse of death, the spiritual death which disconnected Adam and Eve from God, the life-giving power source?" We can find the answer in the words of Jesus:

> For God so loved the world [sinners like us, spiritually disconnected from God] That He gave His only begotten

Son. That whosoever believeth in Him should not perish, but have everlasting life. [Being born again, reconnected to God the power source of all life.]

John 3:16

Life is the opposite word that God spoke to Adam and Eve. To them God said, "You will die." It all began when man believed a lie from Satan who said, "You can be just as clever as God. Why, you don't need Him, make your own decision, don't listen to God."

Jesus came back and paid the penalty for man's disobedience and then said, "If you believe what I tell you, you can have your life back. Re-establish the lifeline between you and God." First of all, I have to understand that God was not talking about dropping dead when He told Adam and Eve they would die. What we understand is that when man becomes alienated from God he is spiritually dead and unable to communicate with God in his sinful state. However, when we receive Jesus in our hearts our spirit becomes born again. We become reconnected with God and we experience a new life. Our father Adam is the one who broke the connection. Since then, every newborn baby has been born spiritually disconnected from God. Only through the sacrifice of Christ then can we become reconnected. Now with our new life in him we remain spiritually connected by following the by-laws of the kingdom. When we don't follow these by-laws we fall in the same trap as our forefather Adam did. We say in fact, "I can do this thing on my own; I don't have to pray and stay in touch. I can do whatever it is I am doing on my own." Disregarding the input we can receive from the Holy Spirit spells failure.

When you are alive in God through Jesus, you relinquish the decision-making process of what is right and wrong to God and walk in His light, or the directions we received from Christ in the sermon on the mount. In this process everything will change for you and the direction of your life will change.

Jesus tells us further that whatever He told us to do was for one purpose only: to restore our life [new life] and to give back our joy. "These things have I spoken unto you, that my joy might remain in you, and that your joy might be full" (John 15:11).

Do you think that perhaps it is painful for God to see how unhappy some of His children are when He made a way for them to be happy every day? Paul and Silas were happy even when they were sitting in jail. Why? You see, the joy that comes from Christ to us cannot be dampened by circumstances or events. Happy family members of the God family walk around all day with that silly grin on their faces. You don't even know why you feel so happy. You're just happy; that's all.

Jesus says, "Do what I tell you to do and you will have the same joy and power to over come and live abundantly as I lived.

> You have not chosen me, but I have chosen you, and ordained you, that you should go and bring forth fruit, and that your fruit should remain: that what soever ye shall ask of the Father in my name He may give it you.
>
> John 15:16

Jesus says, "Look, it was my decision to come here and give you another chance to experience the kind of life God had in mind for you from the beginning. All it really takes, is for you to do what I have told you. Doing what I tell you to do opens unlimited options for you. God is ready and waiting to see if you will commit your life to become a part of the God family." [Which by the way does not mean a member of a church.]

"But when the Comforter is come, whom I will send unto you from the Father, even the Spirit of truth, which proceed from the Father, He shall testify of me" (John 15:26).

Jesus said not to worry, because you will receive this new life in connecting your spirit to God's spirit through the Holy Spirit. The Holy Spirit will be God living in you. He will always remind you to do the right thing. Make your decision today to live the rest of your life according to the sermon on the mount. Decide today that Satan will never steal your joy away from you ever again, because you will never believe his deception. I took this legal document, that I prepared with the help of the Holy Spirit and placed it on my refrigerator. Now I lay my hands on it every time I walk past the refrigerator to remind myself and the Devil, that I know who I am. I also know Satan's tricks and he has put the last one over on me a long time ago. No longer will I fall into the same trap as Papa Adam and Mama Eve, not while I walk in the authority of the word of God.

Reconnected to my Father God, I am happy now. Happy that I don't have to be concerned about tomorrow. Even if every thing around me had to go wrong, even if nothing is working right, I still have that assurance from my Father that He cares for me every minute of every day. Within every situation is the Holy Spirit, who will instruct and guide me through it, and if necessary, my Father will dispatch angels on my behalf. Now I can be happy and stay happy immaterial as to how bleak the situation appears to me.

Legal Document

Restraining Order by the Supreme Judge of the Universe

This order issued in the court of Heaven to bring justice to a family member/s of the judge, who has been unjustly accused and lied about and robbed of his/her joy and heavenly blessings by Satan.

Issued the: ________day of ________ , ________.

In Defense Of: (Write the names of all the family members here.)

____

a. Justifiable evidence has been submitted to the high court of Heaven that Satan has without cause or justifiable reason threatened to induce illness, despondency, sadness, unbelief, fear, unemployment, financial difficulties and other despicable circumstances to intimidate the above family members of God's invisible kingdom.

b. Satan has further intimidated the above named family members by twisting the truth about their Father God and their elder brother Jesus Christ, sending them false messages saying that God did not care about them. Furthermore, Satan pretended that he held power over their circumstances.

c. This investigation was conducted in their defense by the Holy Spirit who was with them at all times, never leaving their side, confirming the fact that Satan has overstepped his authority that was revoked by Christ at the cross of Calvary, when the entire human race was offered redemption at no cost.

d. Orders are hereby issued that the thief should return sevenfold what was stolen.

e. All accusations shall be declared null and void, due to the fact that Satan has been cast out of heaven and ordered by God to yield to the authority of all God's children. Luke 10:17–19

f. These family members and children of God are entitled to receive their blessings according to their own faith, first under the Abrahamic Covenant. Deuteronomy 28. Second under a new and better covenant, re-affirmed by the living Christ who shed his own blood to include even the most violent offenders to become a part of the family of God. John 3:16, Philippians 4:19, Hebrews 8:6, 3 John 2.

Defendant's signature below affirms faithfully that he/she is a family member of God Himself and His son, Jesus Christ, accepting the above conditions and pledge never to allow Satan any opportunity to defeat them again. But will stand fast on the Word of God according to Ephesians 6:13–17 and Galatians 3:13–14. They also pledge to stand on their testimony, Revelation 12:11. Without delay they will approach the Judge directly who has given them access to His chambers through their Personal Representative if any further attempts are made by the enemy, Hebrews 10:19–20. Signatures of the redeemed parties:

Signature: ______________________________ Date: ____________

Signature: ______________________________ Date: ____________

Schedule Revival/Seminar

After reading this book you may feel inspired to schedule a revival/teaching seminar at your church to train your church members how to hear the voice of God and be used by God in the operational gifts of the Holy Spirit. Paul tells us in Philippians 2:5: "Let this mind be in you, which was also in Christ Jesus." This profound statement can change the life of the believer from passive to walking in the powers of the invisible. From being a nominal, boring and unfulfilled as a Christian to one who is living from moment to moment. Having the mind of Christ means that you don't fear the storm but command it to be calm. You don't fear circumstances; you command them to change. You don't fear sickness or cancer or what the devil can do because the mind of Christ is never subject to fear but relies on the invisible power of God that is always at work in the believer through the same Spirit that lived in Christ Jesus. Romans 8:11: "But if the Spirit of him that raised up Jesus from the dead dwell in you, he that raised up Christ from the dead shall also quicken your mortal bodies by his Spirit that dwelleth in you." Your church can be filled with seekers after truth, which may consist of drug dealers and sinners from every walk of life. Once your church has learned the secret of walking and living in the mind of Christ, exciting, eventful, unexpected and very powerful changes will become the norm.

To schedule your future in leading a life in the supernatural, email: Corrie Joubert: faithwalkers@peoplepc.com.